MANY CULTURES, ONE TEAM

Build Your Cultural Repertoire

first edition

Catherine Mercer Bing

Published by:
Technics Publications, LLC
2 Lindsley Road
Basking Ridge, NJ 07920 USA

http://www.TechnicsPub.com

Cover design by Mark Brye

DISCLAIMER:

The material in this book is intended for informational and educational purposes only. No
expressed or implied guarantee as to the effects of the use of the recommendations or
practices can be given nor liability taken.

ISBN, print ed.   9781634620031

ISBN, Kindle ed.   9781634620048

ISBN, ePub ed.   9781634620055

First Printing 2015

Library of Congress Control Number: 2014954485

Global competition is fierce, and the timeframe within which businesses maintain their competitive advantage is now counted in months rather than years. One important source of competitive advantage is human behavior. Team leaders that manage the subtle, but powerful, forces of group dynamics and culture achieve better business outcomes. Team leaders that fail to identify and manage these subtle forces in real-time risk having their plans thwarted.

"Many Cultures, One Team" is based on Cass Mercer Bing's extensive experience helping virtual and multi-cultural teams achieve their full potential. "Many Cultures, One Team" provides extensive advice for team leaders and consultants in a ready-to-use format. It is a crucial guide to anyone who wishes to gain a better handle on a crucial source of competitive advantage: human dynamics on global and virtual teams.

Dr. Amitai Touval, Zicklin School of Business

My favorite part is the case box. It raises questions and makes me think, 'darn, I don't really know!'... The explanations tend to give me a 'Yes, yes, I know' feeling.

Gert Jan Hofstede, Associate Professor at Wageningen UR, The Netherlands

In her new book "Many Cultures, One Team," author Cass Mercer Bing has correctly identified the key to team performance as being team process. In business to date, team process is defined in frameworks that do not sufficiently account for cultural differences. These frameworks are offered in the context of **what** we want to accomplish; change management frameworks for implementing change, project management frameworks for projects, and information technology frameworks for implementing IT projects. But if the change management framework calls for engaging stakeholders, **how** can you accomplish this if you do not understand the Power Distance or Need for Certainty among those stakeholders? If the project management framework calls for chartering and team engagement, **how** do you know what to do if you do not understand the Individualism and Quality of Life orientations of your team members? Enter "Many Cultures, One Team," which lays out complete definitions, real world examples, and practical solutions for tipping the odds of success in your favor. It is not that methodologies such as Agile/Scrum, PMI, or CMI need to be modified or replaced. The knowledge Cass Mercer Bing offers has to be added to and applied in the context of these approaches. It is essential reading for all who lead, or, aspire to lead, diverse and global teams.

Erik Granered, Author of "Global Call Centers: Achieving Outstanding Customer Service Across Cultures and Time Zones"

"Many Cultures, One Team," is a book for today's visionary-pragmatic managers, internal practitioners and all those consultants and learning facilitators following up the development of their organizations into sustainable transformation processes including business partnership strategies. Catherine is providing practical tools and relevant experiences to effectively integrate culture and daily/strategic management with better results.

Sergio Gardelliano, Lic. Sustainable Organizational Transformation
International Consultancy & Learning Facilitation, Vienna, Austria

Catherine has produced a truly groundbreaking handbook and toolkit for designing world-class teams. "Many Cultures, One Team" is unique in its presumption that team members are different, they are affected by their own cultural norms and those of their organizations, and it is absolutely essential for team members to mutually adapt to each other's needs and perspectives!

In most organizations, people are placed on a team and "wished well." "Many Cultures, One Team" illustrates how this frequently dooms a team to at-best mediocre results. The book does a masterful job of combining practical questions and tips to consider with specific roadmaps and tools to develop team members and leaders while also developing the organization so that it may best support and enable the success of its teams. The sections on the Culture in the Workplace Questionnaire™ and the Global Team Process Questionnaire™ are especially valuable since they provide tools by which a team may further develop itself in culturally-adaptive ways.

Peter Bye, President of MDB Group

One of the most challenging aspects of global organizations is creating and leading cross cultural global teams including business units, functional teams, project teams, divisions, etc. It requires an understanding of the complex dynamics of the mental operating systems and cultural preferences of individuals in global organizations. Too often, leaders approach global teams thru their own lens of cultural bias or reference without regard for those of the team members.

Cass has presented a framework for global leaders to go beyond their own comfort zone allowing leaders to recognize and appreciate the cultural challenges involved in leading cross cultural teams. The leader is able to recognize and identify the cultural dynamics and utilize these techniques and strategies in making the organization function more effectively. This approach and the techniques outlined can be applied at multiple levels in the organization which makes a compelling case for leaders and HR professionals who operate in the complex network of cultural behavioral preferences present in global teams.

John E. Warren III, Global Human Resources Executive

Contents at a Glance

Table of Contents

In multi-cultural teams while common purpose and goals are held in common, different approaches are more likely the norm. The strategies listed in the chapters in Part II are focused on national culture (cultural drivers of behavior) and are designed to give team leaders and team members culturally-appropriate approaches as they conduct team interactions, rather than always using "common approaches."

Teams are wonderfully various in composition, purpose, and form, and they exist in almost all organizations. Someday someone will write the taxonomy of teams, but I have a more practical goal: **To help teams work more effectively for their organizations and for the team members.**

Team Issues

You are a senior internal or external consultant specializing in creating effective team interventions. A client comes to you and during the conversation asks for team building training for members of a globally dispersed technology team. The client is convinced that members are not committed to the work of the team even though the outcomes are very important to the success of that division of the company. He points to missed milestone deliverables and a lack of urgency about meeting deadlines.

In a conversation to uncover examples of the problems on the team, the client writes, "*...broadly speaking we have seen the following:*

- *Lack of motivation/initiative*
- *Lack of confidence*
- *Lack of ability to work independently*
- *Lack of taking ownership*
- *Lack of domain knowledge*
- *Inadequate technology skills.*"

In discussions with the team members, they believe that the team leader is not committed to the success of the team. They complain that the team leader:

- Is not keeping team members informed of project updates.
- Is not available during their work hours because they are not all located in the same time zone.
- Gives assignments that develop skills to those employees co-located with the team leader.
- Has never visited their site even though their section was acquired over five years ago.

About the Book

This book is an essential aid for anyone who leads, is a member of, consults with, or supports global teams. The purpose of this book is to give team leaders, team members, and consultants information about where to look to help identify what might be the cause of problems with teams.

The content addresses organizational practices as well as team member cultural orientations and how these impact (negatively or positively) the success of the team. It speaks to employee engagement, improved productivity, and human process interactions (HPIs) on teams. It challenges team leaders and team members to reflect on their cultural assumptions—to improve their cultural metacognition. The book starts with the impact on the team of various organizational practices and continues through the team lifecycle (the team charter, team meetings, celebration of the team's accomplishments) with a specific focus on the impact of culturally driven attitudes, beliefs, and behaviors.

The case stories, examples, and strategy suggestions are the result of collective experiences over the past 25 years. These are real, and most of the stories are examples of teams that have stumbled or those who did not meet their deliverables on time or at/under budget. The Whole Team Support System Framework is introduced in Part I, and the questions at the end of the sections are designed to help the reader seek the root causes of organizational practices that may cause issues that impact team success.

As you can imagine there are specific types of issues for each type of team. Since we cannot possibly deal with all the types of issues for the wide variety of teams, the focus here is on cross-cultural project management teams. These are common types of teams in many organizations. They also have the highest level of complexity, primarily due to cultural differences, functional boundaries, and likelihood that some members are not co-located.

Katzenbach and Smith, in *The Wisdom of Teams*, define effective teams as:

> *...a small number of people with complementary skills who are committed to a common purpose, performance goals, and approach for which they hold themselves mutually accountable.*

Acknowledgements

This book never would have been written if Artie Mahal had not asked me to write a chapter in his book *Facilitator's and Trainer's Toolkit: Engage and Energize Participants for Success in Meetings, Classes and Workshops*. We were talking about the work I do (cross-cultural consulting) and I mentioned the "Team Leader Tool Kit" we had created to sell to clients. When Artie saw it he suggested that it might be more effective at marketing the company and the capability in book form. He offered to introduce me to Steve Hoberman (Technics Publications), who agreed to publish my book.

I want to thank my husband, John W. Bing, not only for doing the first copy editing, but more importantly for introducing me to the world of cultural differences. He is the founder of our business and has the personal relationships with Geert Hofstede, on whose research our consulting business is centered. Without his support and backing, I never would have found time or the focus to start much less finish this book.

I want to acknowledge all the staff members who ever have worked at ITAP and those current employees (Ann, Linda and Amitai) who supported me throughout the many years of our working together. I want to especially thank Ann Dougherty whose creativity framed a lot of the kinds of materials used in this book. She also is a terrific editor and proofreader and she made sure I was accurate in my analysis of what cultural drivers were at play in various situations.

Finally, I want to thank both Geert Hofstede and his son, Gert Jan; Geert for his important work in the field that allowed us to create our business (John and I appreciate the friendship and guidance Geert has given us over the years) and Gert Jan who was very gracious in giving me sound advice about how to make this a much better book.

While I am grateful to all of the above, any errors in the book are mine alone.

Who is more committed...the team leader or the team members? Are there cultural issues on this team? Could there be performance issues? Can you tell which of these problems might be exacerbated by organizational alignment or organizational practices? Are the team members interacting effectively? Is the team leader capable of leading a multi-cultural team?

This real life example demonstrates some of the complexities that teams face. A variety of factors here negatively affect team success. They include, but are not limited to:

- Remote selection practices (not knowing which foreign university degrees actually prepare remote employees with "adequate technical skills")

- Organizational policies (budget constraints) that limit travel to remote locations

- Misunderstanding of the leadership needs of the employees (for example, how much context and specific directions to give them when delegating)

- Lack of appreciation for the needs of the employees to have more accessibility to the remote supervisor

- Limited foresight as to the impact on both employee development and employee motivation when interesting assignments are distributed.

Teams, because they represent significant corporate investment, require proactive attention and continued support. Many teams are multi-cultural just by the nature of today's workforce. Success requires early detection of and response to obstacles pressuring the teams from outside or from within. To prevent these difficulties from hindering the team's productivity and effectiveness, proper identification of what can derail even the most dedicated team is essential to creating high-performing multi-cultural teams.

As companies strive to improve their global reach through the use of teams, two factors are critical to that goal:

1. Technical Expertise: Such as research, finance, sales, marketing, project management, general management, and

2. Human Process Expertise: How teams interact to establish clear goals, communicate across national and cultural boundaries and time zones, solve problems, work together as well as independently, and resolve differences. Actions in all these areas are, at least in part, culturally defined.

Of course technical / functional approaches are also impacted by culture. Dr. Marieke de Moojj has written about the impact of culture on the advertising and marketing in her books *Global Marketing and Advertising; Understanding Cultural Paradoxes and Consumer Behavior and Culture: Consequences for Global Marketing and Advertising.*

Significant corporate Human Resource efforts focus on hiring and compensating the best technically qualified people, some of whom become members of global teams. It is too often assumed that technical expertise is all that matters. When we look at teams that miss milestones or deadlines, we often see two equally qualified employees produce widely different quality or quantity of work. Therefore, other factors obviously are playing a role.

If global teams, which represent significant corporate investments towards important goals, receive the attention and support of management, their chance for success is magnified. Such support can provide early detection of and response to looming obstacles in order to prevent them from hindering the team's productivity and effectiveness. Global team leader development, combined with focused team process monitoring and support, significantly improves team effectiveness.

Employees require knowledge, skills, information, competencies, resources, motivation and incentives to perform tasks. They will fail to the extent that these elements are missing or less than optimal (for example if they are not culturally appropriate). A relationship between process and performance exists on teams. At the most basic level, it should be obvious that dissatisfied team members are more likely to contribute less to team productivity.

HOW THE BOOK IS ORGANIZED

In the first ten books on teams that I looked at to start my research, I realized that not one of them included how organizational practices **external** to the team can be a barrier to team success. This book fills this important niche.

This book also helps readers build their cultural repertoire. The strategies in the chapters exist to provide information about what kinds of team activities are more effective with people who have specific cultural orientations. These are meant as options for team leaders and members to help them embrace behavioral diversity by giving them alternative ways to be more effective with each other. These lists are not intended to be prescriptive but to give readers tools and approaches to help them understand why what they are currently doing works sometimes but may not work all the time or with all team members.

The basis of the contents of the book comes from:

- A breadth of understanding of the pressures on global, multi-cultural teams (from within the team and from outside the team or from the organization)

- Creating applications to measure human process interactions (HPIs) on teams and administering these assessments to hundreds of teams

- Consulting about dysfunctional teams and providing consulting interventions and training to improve productivity

- Leading large, cross-functional, multi-cultural teams

- Building practices based on the work of Dr. Geert Hofstede, the pioneer in comparative intercultural research.

The book starts with an introduction to cultural dimensions identified by Dr. Geert Hofstede and the two orientations associated with each dimension. Contained in the four sections outlined below are an examination of external and internal factors that impact team success, recommendations, ideas and suggestions for team interventions, activities and assessments as well as a list of resources. Each section may be more or less valuable for particular audiences.

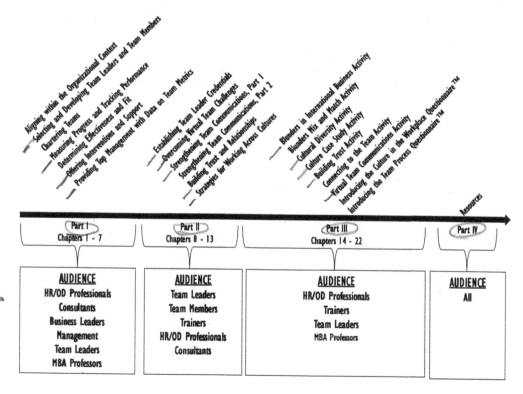

I.   **External Factors (Organizational Practices) that Impact Team Success:** The first section of this book looks at the organization as a whole in order to help the reader ensure that organizational barriers and bridges to building productive teams are identified. In it I introduce the Whole Team Support Framework and devote one chapter to each segment of the Framework. Chapters end with a series of questions that can be used to diagnose problem areas.

- Chapter 1 – Aligning within the Organizational Context
- Chapter 2 – Selecting and Developing Team Leaders and Team Members
- Chapter 3 – Chartering Teams
- Chapter 4 – Measuring Progress and Tracking Performance
- Chapter 5 – Determining Effectiveness and Fit
- Chapter 6 – Offering Interventions and Support
- Chapter 7 – Providing Top Management with Data on Team Metrics

AUDIENCE: This part is most useful for Human Resources (HR)/Organizational Development (OD) specialists or consultants, business leaders, graduate school professors and somewhat useful for team leaders.

II.   **Internal (National) Cultural Factors that Impact Team Success:** The second section of the book offers approaches to consider for management, team leaders, and team members to improve team performance. Included in each section are stories of either team problems or successes as well as lists of strategies aligned with particular cultural orientations. These lists are intended to offer alternatives to help teams build their repertoire of culturally varied approaches.

- Chapter 8 – Establishing Team Leader Credentials
- Chapter 9 – Overcoming Virtual Team Challenges
- Chapter 10 – Strengthening Team Communications, Part 1
- Chapter 11 – Strengthening Team Communications, Part 2
- Chapter 12 – Building Trust and Relationships
- Chapter 13 – Strategies for Working Across Cultures

AUDIENCE: This part is most useful for management, team leaders, team members, trainers/facilitators and HR/OD professionals.

III.   **Many Cultures One Team Activities—Tools and Techniques:** The third part includes Instructor Guides to team activities for cross-cultural and virtual teams, intervention ideas to help readers improve team process and performance, and recommended instruments for measuring cultural profiles and human process interactions (HPIs).

- Chapter 14 – Blunders in International Business Activity (for in-person team meetings) designed to establish the importance of cultural differences in business.
- Chapter 15 – Blunders Mix and Match Activity (for virtual team meetings). This activity is a version of the previous activity modified for use in virtual team meetings.

- Chapter 16 – Cultural Diversity Activity designed to improve cultural diversity metacognition.
- Chapter 17 – Culture Case Study Activity designed to give an example of how cultural orientations may intersect and overlap in real business situations. It also can be used to measure how well members can identify behavioral characteristics of various cultural orientations.
- Chapter 18 – Building Trust Activity designed to identify what builds, breaks or is a barrier to trust on teams.
- Chapter 19 – Connecting to the Team Activity designed to help build relationships on the team.
- Chapter 20 – Virtual Team Communications Activity designed to get the conversation started about how to set communication protocols and determine each team members' preferred technology. This speeds and smoothes virtual communication.
- Chapter 21 – Introducing the Culture in the Workplace Questionnaire™. This is an instrument used to measure and report on the respondent's personal cultural profile. It also can be used to create team profiles and for research.
- Chapter 22 – Introducing the Team Process Questionnaire™ System. This includes three instruments for global, mono-cultural, and action learning teams to measure human process interactions.

AUDIENCE: This part is most useful for HR/OD professionals, trainers, team leaders, team members, trainers/facilitators.

IV. Resources: The final section includes a bibliography.

really?!

Dr. Geert Hofstede, a Dutch social scientist, created the field of comparative intercultural studies. He is Director (Emeritus) of the Institute for Research on Intercultural Cooperation (IRIC) at the University of Maastricht, the Netherlands. Dr. Hofstede's pioneering study of IBM affiliates in fifty countries, elaborated in his book *Culture's Consequences*, helped to form the foundation of the field of comparative cultures. In *Culture's Consequences*, Dr. Hofstede analyzed how workplace values are influenced by culture. Over 200 subsequent studies validating his earlier results have included, among many others, commercial airline pilots, students in 23 countries, civil service managers in 14 countries, and high-income consumers in 15 countries.

Hofstede can be regarded as one of the leading representatives of intercultural research and studies. According to The Wall Street Journal, Geert Hofstede is the 16th top influential business thinker in the world, "based on Google hits, media mentions and academic citations."[1]

The findings of his research and his theoretical ideas are used worldwide in both psychology and management studies. His more recent book co-authored by Gert Jan Hofstede and Michael Minkov (the third edition of *Culture and Organizations: Software of the Mind*) examines what drives people apart, even when it seems obvious that cooperation would be in the interest of everyone. His book examines society's unwritten rules and explores how national cultures differ.

Cultural differences come from patterns for thinking, feeling, and potential acting learned in childhood and practiced throughout our lives. Once these patterns are established, they must be unlearned before being able to learn something different. Values learned at a very early age are deeply held, often unconscious, and the most difficult to unlearn. Mental software or culture for a group is the aggregate of those patterns of thinking, feeling, and acting.

For example, imagine a child in school who is misbehaving. What would you define as "misbehavior"? In your experience, who gets the blame for his/her misbehavior – the

---

[1] New Breed of Business Gurus Rises, By Erin White, May 5, 2008.

parents, the child, the school? How is the blame administered? The answers to these questions may vary by culture and these practices are later reproduced in the workplace.

What we are not talking about is "organizational culture/climate." Reichers and Schneider (1990) define organizational climate as "...shared perceptions of organizational policies, practices, and procedures [within an organization]." These are not learned when we are young and are not deeply held beliefs or patterns, as evidenced by our ability to move from one organization to another. Instead, in this book, what others call organizational culture is referred to as "organizational practices" which is meant to include practices, procedures, and policies.

Culture, what Dr. Hofstede defines as "software of the mind or mental programming," is one of the variables that guides peoples' actions and reactions. Understanding one's own culture and the impact of culture on the actions of others is essential for effective global team interactions.

The cultural terminology used in this book will refer to Hofstede's model with the updated and simplified terms used in the Culture in the Workplace Questionnaire™ (CWQ) application.

If you are already familiar with the work of Geert Hofstede, you have noticed that we are using different terminology in this section. There are notes after the definitions and examples which list the original Hofstede terms.

INDIVIDUALISM DIMENSION

Individualism (the dimension) is the degree to which decisions are made for the benefit of the individual or the benefit of the group. Individualism has two orientations, **Individual Orientation** or **Group Orientation**. Different cultural groups will define the qualities and characteristics of an effective team member based on their cultural orientation. They may either prefer a more linear work flow—I do my work and pass it off to you (**Individual Orientation**)—or a more collaborative effort, where we work on it together—I help you and you help me (**Group Orientation**).

In teams, those who exhibit behaviors associated with Individual Orientation may appear to those with a Group Orientation as loners (they go off and do their work alone) who lack commitment to the success of the team. Those who exhibit behaviors associated with Group Orientation may be perceived as unable to make decisions on their own and may be perceived as not qualified (especially when it appears that they need others to help them).

Original Hofstede terms:

- DIMENSION: Individualism

- ORIENTATIONS: Individualism / Individualist or Collectivism / Collectivist.

Here are some approaches to consider when working with those whose orientation is different from yours.

If you have been socialized with values from an Individual Orientation:

- Learn that others will respond after considering the group interests and impact of your expectations...

- ...and that they may expect and require consultation before making or acting on a decision.

- If you meet resistance, passive or active, identify the common interests and outcomes up front; make the collective case.

- Be patient; learn to trust the team to deliver when they have collectively worked out together.

- Know that others may expect you to put the team interests before their or your own self-interests, and that is OK.

If you have been socialized with values from a Group Orientation:

- Learn that people may respond quickly and directly before considering other's input or interests...

- ...and they may expect decisions, and make their own decisions, without waiting to consult others.

- If you are meeting inertia, think about and identify individual outcomes, actions and interests; engage individuals in support of team targets.

- Break down the group objective into individual actions and responsibilities; trust individuals to deliver their portion.

- Know that others may expect you to recognize their and your own interests up front before the team's, and that is OK.

POWER DISTANCE DIMENSION

Power Distance is the degree to which the difference between those in power and the less powerful is accepted. Power Distance has two orientations, **Hierarchical Orientation** or **Participative Orientation**. This dimension affects how people from different cultures would describe the qualities and characteristics of an effective leader very differently—say, China and Great Britain.

People from participative cultures, (even those with a relatively weak Participative Orientation, such as the US) often have a difficult time understanding why anyone would prefer a hierarchical approach. Western practices such as giving 360° feedback (Give feedback to your boss? Not a wise career move in some Hierarchical cultures!) and establishing matrix organizations (not knowing who is really in charge or who has the most power) are acceptable practices from a Western perspective. However, these practices can be confusing at best or career limiting at worst in some hierarchical cultures.

In teams, comfort with hierarchy (not questioning who is in charge, not raising issues to management, not offering ideas different from the team leader) may appear to those with a Participative Orientation as lacking commitment to the team or lacking creativity. Those with a Participative Orientation may be seen by those with Hierarchical Orientation as disloyal to the leader and they may be pegged as "troublemakers" because they are pointing out flaws or recommending changes in how things are done.

Original Hofstede terms:

- DIMENSION: Power Distance

- ORIENTATIONS: Large Power Distance or Small Power Distance.

Here are some approaches to consider when working with those whose orientation is different from yours.

If you have been socialized with values from a Hierarchical Orientation:

- Learn that others expect to be consulted and required to contribute before the decision; that helps make things happen...

- ...so be sensitive to irritation and hang on a bit; ask opinions, encourage ideas, and show that you've taken them seriously.

- They know you have power; you don't have to always use it, so allow others to make decisions and guide them if they go wrong.

- Recognize that others are happy to access the lower levels in the business if that works; your clients may not need you if someone in your team can do it for them.

- Know that others may not see that their loyalty will be reciprocated; they may not trust you to protect them if they take the hit.

If you have been socialized with values from a Participative Orientation:

- Learn that others may expect the boss to tell them what to do; that helps make things happen…

- …so brace yourself and give more up-front direction if people seem frustrated or puzzled by questions and invitations to speak up.

- If you have power, use it more openly, more obviously, more directly; people will respond positively to your lead.

- Be sensitive to other's use of hierarchy as a way to make things happen; your clients may expect you match their hierarchy as the appropriate means of access.

- Know that subordinates (it's OK to call them that) may even take the blame, but will expect you to protect them if they do.

CERTAINTY DIMENSION

Certainty is the extent to which people feel anxiety unless there are rules, regulations, and controls, or are more comfortable with unstructured, ambiguous, or unpredictable situations. The two orientations for the Certainty dimension are **Need for Certainty Orientation** or **Tolerance for Ambiguity Orientation**. (Note: This dimension is not about risk but about anxiety when there is less planning and communication than is preferred.)

Some team members want more information before making a decision (**Need for Certainty Orientation**), and others feel comfortable making a decision with less information (**Tolerance for Ambiguity Orientation**). Those who want more information (Need for Certainty) may feel uncomfortable and may distrust those who seem to want to make quick decisions because it appears that their decisions and actions may not be carefully thought out. Those with a Tolerance for Ambiguity may feel that gathering more information is a waste of time ("analysis paralysis") and they may view others as not competent because they seem unable to get to the work of the project.

Original Hofstede terms:

- DIMENSION: Uncertainty Avoidance

- ORIENTATIONS: Strong Uncertainty Avoidance or Weak Uncertainty Avoidance.

Here are some approaches to consider when working with those whose orientation is different from yours.

If you have been socialized with values from a <u>Need for Certainty Orientation</u>:

- Learn that others may be ready to act with less information than you think they should have; "analysis paralysis" de-motivates...

- ...so brace yourself to allow quicker, less-informed decisions and actions to happen—and focus others on lessons learned.

- Be brief in your reassurance that a given course of action is tried and tested; build the case around questions rather than having all points covered up front.

- Expect and allow creativity based on new ideas and untried methods; even your clients may expect that of you.

- You may need to focus more on improvement rather than accepting the status quo.

If you have been socialized with values from a <u>Tolerance for Ambiguity Orientation</u>:

- Learn that others may expect professionals to provide full and complete information before taking action...

- ...so invest more up front in analysis, information and guidance; even if the parameters are set wide, still set some.

- You may be confident it will work, but that may not be enough to convince others; anticipate their concerns and address them without waiting to be asked.

- Your creativity may generate lots of ideas, but it may leave others puzzled or uneasy; your clients need to know you will deliver.

- You may need to focus more on compliance with procedures and policies.

ACHIEVEMENT DIMENSION

Achievement is the degree to which we focus on goal achievement or have a preference for quality of life and caring for others. The two orientations for the Achievement dimension are **Achievement Orientation** or **Quality of Life Orientation**. In both cases, people want to get things done, but those with a stronger **Quality of Life Orientation** work through relationships, even with people not part of their in-group, to achieve their goals. In cultures with higher Quality of Life country scores (Nordic countries, for example), you will find longer maternity and paternity leave and more weeks of vacation benefits than in countries with a high Achievement Orientation.

Team members who are focused more on goals, competition and winning (**Achievement Orientation**) than on the impact this may have on people may feel it is not fair that they have to work with others (with a Quality of Life Orientation) whom they judge not to be as committed to team success. Those who prefer working with people and working to find win-win scenarios (Quality of Life Orientation) to achieve their goals may find it difficult to work with people who they perceive as uncaring.

Original Hofstede terms:

- DIMENSION: Masculinity

- ORIENTATIONS: Masculinity / Masculine or Femininity / Feminine.

Here are some approaches to consider when working with those whose orientation is different from yours.

If you have been socialized with values from an Achievement Orientation:

- Recognize that not everybody sees the need to subordinate their lives to work; they can deliver and have "quality of life."

- Emphasize humility and modesty in your approach. Focus on continued service to the internal and external customer.

- Recognize quality may be equally important than quantity or speed.

- Stress interdependence and concern for others.

- You may enjoy "constructive conflict," but others may see it as unproductive and part of the problem; harmony can be effective.

If you have been socialized with values from a <u>Quality of Life Orientation</u>:

- Recognize that others may not need you to allow for their wider lives; they will take care of it and will expect the same of you.

- Show drive or ambition for completion of tasks and meeting of deadlines. Communicate and respond with a sense of urgency.

- Deliver what you promise, when you promise, and give more than you promised.

- Stress and reward performance and results.

- Expect more conflict than seems prudent and try to see it and use it as a source of solutions rather than as a problem.

TIME ORIENTATION DIMENSION

Time Orientation is the extent to which members of a society are prepared to adapt to reach a desirable future (pragmatism) or the extent to which they focus on fulfilling their present needs and objectives. The two orientations for the Time dimension are **Long-Term Orientation** or **Short-Term Orientation**. One clear distinction between the two orientations is the focus on profits (**Short-Term Orientation**) vs. market position (**Long-Term Orientation**). Companies in the financial sector (such as banking, insurance, and investment firms) focus on the short-term horizon due to the pressures of quarterly earnings reports.

Too often teams are pressed to get it done now, and even if they can only achieve 80% of their objectives, that is seen as good enough (Short-Term Orientation). Those who work to the 80% may be perceived as lacking attention to quality or customer needs by those with Long-Term Orientation.

Those with a Long-Term Orientation may approach their projects or tasks with the attitude that it is worth it to put in the time to get it right, even if it delays the deliverables. They may be ostracized and often criticized by those with a Short-Term Orientation for impeding the team's work.

Original Hofstede terms:

- DIMENSION: Long Term Orientation

- ORIENTATIONS: Long Term Orientation or Short Term Orientation.

Here are some approaches to consider when working with those whose orientation is different from yours.

If you have been socialized with values from a **Long-Term Orientation**:

- Recognize that others may be expecting and requiring results soon—or even now; look for quick-wins that address that need...

- ...so track back from the longer horizons to identify the shorter-term deliverables that are important for long-term success.

- Know that others may expect frequent and quick recognition for specific achievements rather than waiting for long-term outcomes.

- Others may expect a reliance on past and recent experience to frame or drive tactics for the next phase rather than developing new methodologies for markets that may not exist yet.

- Use measures that focus on profit and near-term success to identify and articulate the longer-term trends.

If you have been socialized with values from a **Short-Term Orientation**:

- Recognize that others may be less concerned with delivery now and more focused on tomorrow's issues and needs...

- ...so stress the mid/long-term benefits as well as the short-term wins.

- Know that others may expect the value of their long-term focus to be recognized as much as those who deliver now.

- While recognizing near-term delivery may be necessary, others may be requiring you to focus "ahead of the curve" by ensuring the resources and planning are in place to meet the needs of the market long term.

- Introduce and maintain measures that track and recognize long-term success, linking with data that tracks today's output.

INDULGENCE DIMENSION

Indulgence is defined as a tendency to allow for relatively free gratification of basic human drives related to enjoying life and having fun or the conviction that such gratification needs to be regulated by strict social norms. The orientations are **Indulgence Orientation** or **Restraint Orientation**. The differences relate to whether one acts as

Puritanical

one pleases, spends, or indulges in leisure and fun-related activities with friends or alone (**Indulgence Orientation**) or has the conviction that such gratification needs to be curbed and regulated by strict social norms (**Restraint Orientation**).[2]

Original Hofstede terms:

- DIMENSION: Indulgence versus Restraint

- ORIENTATIONS: Indulgence/Indulgent or Restraint/Restrained.

Here are some approaches to consider when working with those whose orientation is different from yours.

If you have been socialized with values from an <u>Indulgence Orientation</u>:

- Show your serious side. A sober and austere attitude is a sign of credibility and professionalism in the workplace.

- Demonstrate discretion and prudence. Enthusiasm and vivacity may be mistaken for lack of self-control.

- Don't be surprised if when you smile at someone in greeting, they do not return your greeting in kind. Smiling may be suspect. Expect instead a neutral face and a sober demeanor.

- Expect that others may be more reticent and guarded in their interpersonal interactions. This does not mean they are unapproachable.

- Recognize that for others, maintaining order is key.

If you have been socialized with values from a <u>Restraint Orientation</u>:

- No matter your inclination or mood, it is expected that your actions and behavior reflect optimism and enthusiasm. Think positive!

- Demonstrate exuberance, energy and cheerfulness. Circumspection could be mistaken for apathy.

- Smile! It is not uncommon to greet both acquaintances and strangers with a smile and pleasant demeanor. For customer service interactions, it is expected.

---

[2] Hofstede, G., Hofstede L.G., Minkov, M. *Cultures and Organizations: Software of the Mind*, quoted with permission.

- Expect that others may be more outgoing, upbeat and open in their interpersonal interactions. This does not mean they lack seriousness.

- Recognize that for others, happiness, a sense of well-being, and freedom of expression are key.

SAMPLE COUNTRY SCORES

Cultural terminology provides non-threatening language that is useful when talking about differences or similarities in behavioral approaches. The Hofstede dimensions are value neutral, without judgment of which side of the orientation dichotomy is better.

In this book it is deliberate in that there is rarely naming of countries with particular orientations (scores) in an effort to avoid stereotyping. After all, just because the country score indicates a certain orientation, that is not predictive about all individuals from that culture. People from the same culture can have very different cultural orientations depending on where they were raised, how they were raised, and by whom. The country score is a collective result, and since culture is by definition a shared phenomenon, an individual cannot be a culture. However, individuals can and do demonstrate culturally-based behavioral preferences. It is these preferences that are articulated and explained by the Hofstede model of culture.

The Hofstede cultural dimensions are a framework, a starting point from which to analyze the behaviors of others. This book offers a straightforward view of how the orientations may impact workplace behaviors and offers strategies on how to respond.

The country score is a valid first-reference to help anticipate the preferences of people from different cultures when there is no prior knowledge about them. The country score provides a basis for determining appropriate action but behaviors can (and should) be adapted in the light of experience with and observation of other individuals.

What is most helpful is developing the ability to recognize behaviors that indicate a preference for one orientation or the other of a cultural dimension. Only in recognizing specific behaviors in self and others can one be more likely to act and respond appropriately.

If a person's preference is for a particular cultural orientation, it does not mean that the individual will always or even usually behave that way. People learn to adapt – and may be able to sustain it, even if they don't like it. However, their "preference" will most likely remain constant and in their consciousness.

Each side of a dimension can be a strength or become a vulnerability in a cross-cultural environment. What may be advantageous in one situation may be a hindrance in another; what counts is what level of self-awareness a person can bring to different situations – and through that self-awareness, the person's ability to adapt appropriately even if it means they sometimes behave in a manner which is far from their culturally-based preference.

How each cultural orientation manifests itself may differ slightly from one culture to another.

To help think about the differences in country cultures please see the results charted below. Each of these spidergrams represents the country scores as measured in Geert Hofstede's research. The charts below are listed in the following order. First are the BRIC countries (Brazil, Russia, India and China) because these often are of most interest as important emerging markets. A few other countries are listed for comparison. These, listed in alphabetical order, include Argentina, Germany, Japan, Singapore, South Korea and the US.

The spokes are the dimensions that were introduced previously.

1. As you can see, for example, Russia, China, and Singapore have relatively high Power Distance scores. This indicates a strong Hierarchical Orientation. When the Power Distance score is low, this indicates a strong Participative Orientation.

2. Scores over 50 on the second spoke indicate the Need for Certainty. Brazil, Russia, Argentina, Japan, and South Korea have strong Need for Certainty scores.

3. For the spoke at the top of the spidergram (Individualism) you can see that the US has the highest score (Individual Orientation). It is helpful to remember that over two thirds of the countries in the database have Group Orientation scores.

(For a full description of the research on which these scores are based, please see *Culture and Organizations; Software of the Mind* [3rd edition] by Geert Hofstede, Gert Jan Hofstede and Michael Minkov.)

Brazil Scores

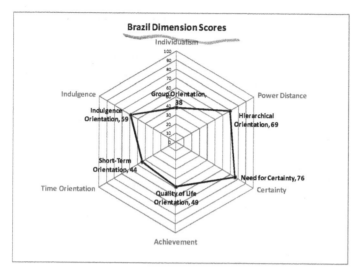

38 — Group Orientation

69 — Hierarchical Orientation

76 — Need for Certainty Orientation

49 — Quality of Life Orientation

44 — Short-Term Orientation

59 — Indulgence Orientation

Russia Scores

39 — Group Orientation

93 — Hierarchical Orientation

95 — Need for Certainty Orientation

36 — Quality of Life Orientation

81 — Long-Term Orientation

20 — Restraint Orientation

India Scores

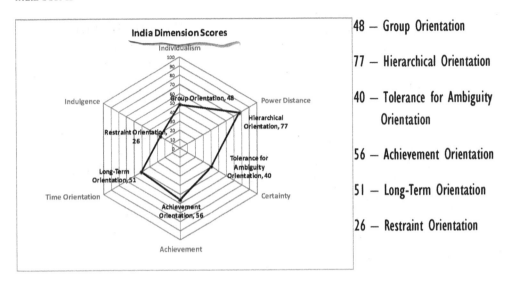

48 — Group Orientation

77 — Hierarchical Orientation

40 — Tolerance for Ambiguity
Orientation

56 — Achievement Orientation

51 — Long-Term Orientation

26 — Restraint Orientation

China Scores

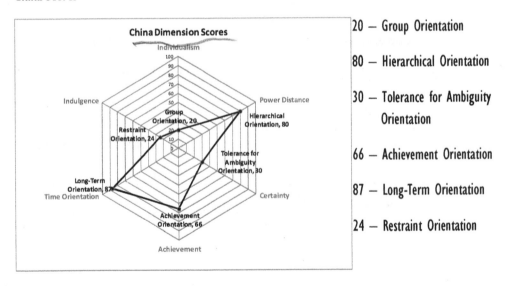

20 — Group Orientation

80 — Hierarchical Orientation

30 — Tolerance for Ambiguity
Orientation

66 — Achievement Orientation

87 — Long-Term Orientation

24 — Restraint Orientation

Argentina Scores

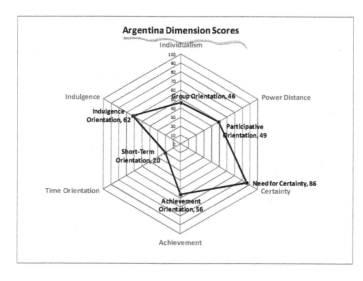

46 — Group Orientation

49 — Participative Orientation

86 — Need for Certainty Orientation

56 — Achievement Orientation

20 — Short-Term Orientation

62 — Indulgence Orientation

Germany Scores

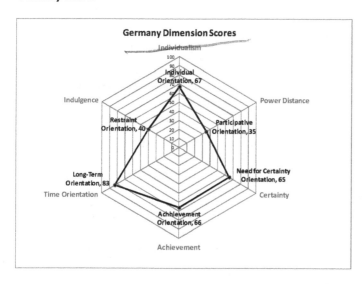

67 — Individual Orientation

35 — Participative Orientation

65 — Need for Certainty Orientation

66 — Achievement Orientation

83 — Long-Term Orientation

40 — Restraint Orientation

Japan Scores

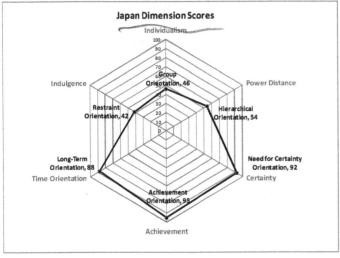

46 — Group Orientation

54 — Hierarchical Orientation

92 — Need for Certainty Orientation

95 — Achievement Orientation

88 — Long-Term Orientation

42 — Restraint Orientation

Singapore Scores

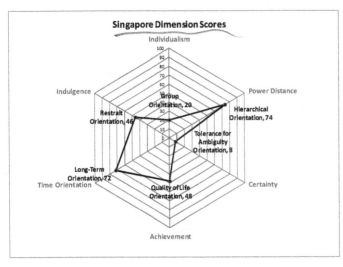

20 — Group Orientation

74 — Hierarchical Orientation

8 — Tolerance for Ambiguity Orientation

48 — Quality of Life Orientation

72 — Long-Term Orientation

46 — Restraint Orientation

South Korea Scores

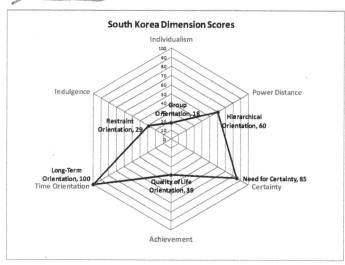

18 — Group Orientation

60 — Hierarchical Orientation

85 — Need for Certainty Orientation

39 — Quality of Life Orientation

100 — Long-Term Orientation

29 — Restraint Orientation

US Scores

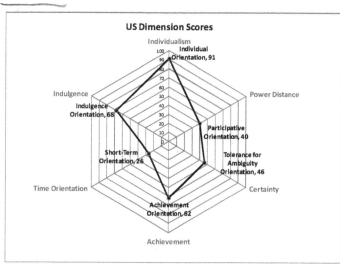

91 — Individual Orientation

40 — Participative Orientation

46 — Tolerance for Ambiguity Orientation

62 — Achievement Orientation

26 — Short-Term Orientation

68 — Indulgence Orientation

Part I
External Cultural Factors that Impact Team Success

Too often, teams—even mission critical ones—are pulled together in haste and the success of the team is left to the team leader. There are both internal and external factors that contribute to team success or failure, much of which is out of the team leader's span of control:

- External factors such as compensation packages and reporting structures can be categorized as things related to organizational practices.

- Internal factors may include processes the team uses, communications between team members, and work handoff, which may be within the span of control of the team leader, and behavioral drivers that are not necessarily within the team leader's control but he/she may need to manage.

Funding

A major, global pharmaceutical company made a company-wide finance reporting change. They moved the monies from the compound development research team leader's budget and reallocated the monies into functional leaders' budgets. This was an attempt by headquarters to get better forecasting and budget reporting figures.

Impact on the Team

Team interactions started falling apart. The team leader was faced with a team that was becoming less productive. Team members' priorities changed from team to departmental goals. When the funding was moved, team members felt that this change signaled that management prioritized departmental work over their work on team goals. Also, since it would be the functional leaders, rather than the team leader, who made salary and bonus decisions, the attention was redirected away from the work of the team to their other functional responsibilities. This organizational change refocused team members' priorities on their departmental work rather than on their research.

When measuring team interactions, research shows that too often teams are doomed to struggle due to external factors (such as organizational arrangements) or internal factors (such as personal values/different ways of approaching team tasks) outside the control of the team and team leader.

Typically, organizations look first (and often only) at internal factors when team deliverables are derailed. There is an assumption that there is something wrong within the team, and even then they rarely take into consideration cultural orientations as behavioral drivers. There are approaches of team leaders and team members related to national cultural values that team leaders cannot control but would be more effective if he/she understood and addressed them.

Team members often have functional responsibilities outside the team. All sorts of organizational issues either support a team environment or make success on teams more difficult:

- Is the organizational culture one that supports and recognizes team effort (group recognition) or individual efforts of team members? If the organization focuses solely on the individual achievements, team members may compete, hoard information, and refuse to share or collaborate.

- Who conducts performance assessments of team members? Employees will attend to the priorities of whoever has the power to fire them and to assess their performance.

- Who makes salary/bonus decisions based on the work within the team? In Achievement- or Individual-orientated culture, employees will focus on how to increase their salary and bonus.

- How are teams funded—through departments/functional budgets? As in the example above, funding salaries and other resources will focus employee priorities.

- How are team members expected to handle multiple priorities when the priorities of the team and the priorities in the department conflict? If the team leader and the functional leader do not work this out, it is likely to cause conflicts or at least tensions.

If we want teams to be successful, we need to look at the systems within which the teams are going to operate as well as the interactions within the teams themselves. The external/organizational factors that impact team success to review include those in the Whole Team Support System Framework.

This Framework is useful for those who take an organizational view of how to support teams. These are likely to include business leaders, Organizational Development Specialists, Consultants and Human Resources professionals. Each heading in the Framework lists actions that support team success.

Whole Team Support Framework

This part of the book will review each of these areas in detail. In addition, chapters will include lists of questions to ask in order to identify the negative effects of (and perhaps eliminate some of) the external and organizational pressures on teams.

Those responsible for the success of the team need to attend to details that may impact the output of the team and the way the team members work together. Alignment is perhaps the most critical step in ensuring team effectiveness.

How can one be a productive worker in an unproductive system? How can team leaders and team members succeed in a system that is not structured for team success? Won't team members pay more attention to the work that will be considered in their performance reviews? Won't they read into corporate changes messages that may not be intended? Won't they pay more attention to their work instead of collaborating if the rewards and recognition programs focus on individual achievements, especially in times of stress or if there is fear of losing their jobs?

Not all of the organizational factors can be controlled, but thinking through the organizational constraints and putting organizational structures in place that one can control may not only start the team off right, but also may support productive results and mitigate problems that otherwise would have come up during the team's work.

Some of the areas to consider include:

- Is the organizational culture team-focused? For example, is teamwork or collaboration expressed in the stated corporate values? If it is expressed as an organizational value, what systems reinforce this commitment? If teaming and collaboration is organizationally expressed as a value, this supports the logic one could use in building a business case for various organizational changes needed to support the teams.

- Do the salary structures and bonus decisions reside with the team leader or the functional leader or both? Many people will focus their work on what is perceived to be of more value, specifically that which is considered during the compensation review.

- Do the performance systems and Key Performance Indicator (KPI) assessments include input from the team leader on the work performed in the team? If not, attention on the work of the team will be perceived as less valuable.

- How are team members and the team leader chosen?

- What criteria should be used in choosing team members? Is it who is the best qualified person or who is the person who has the bandwidth right now to join the work of the team?

- Who makes the decision about who should be included (stakeholder, team leader, functional leader, or some combination)?

- How are people asked/told about their team involvement and responsibilities? In person? In an email? By invitation? By assignment as part of their functional responsibilities? Which is more motivational to the potential team members?

- What are team members told about their authority as a representative of their function on this team? Is it very clear to them whether or not they have the authority to make certain kinds of decisions for their function? It might be seen as an honor to have the authority or responsibility to make decisions that represent their function's perspectives.

- Who asks/tells? Managers who have been socialized with participative values are more likely to ask people to join the team. Leaders with more hierarchical values (see the Power Distance dimension) may assign members to the team and depending on how high in the organization the assignment comes from, the more honor is bestowed.

- Do the senior leaders take the work of the team into account when they make corporate decisions related to team process or to the work of the team?

- Do they communicate with the team or team leader when priorities change to assure the team of the continued importance of their work?

While these may seem like small details, the unintended consequences of not initiating the team's work with these considerations will reverberate throughout the work timeline for the project.

Recognizing the Value of Employees' Work

The leader of a cross-functional team is having difficulties getting certain team members to focus on the work of the team. It is nearing the end of the budget year, and the team leader is concerned that she will not get a bonus because the team is missing milestones. Team members tell her they are busy and cannot spend as much time right now on achieving the outcomes of this team.

Impact on the Team

Since the compensation scheme is such that the bonuses are individual, at the end of the performance year, team member focuses more on individual results than team results because that is what is recognized and rewarded by the organization. The team was not able to complete its deliverables on time.

Here are the questions the reader should be asking to identify whether organizational alignment factors (which are outside the team's control) are negatively impacting the team's performance. If the answers are "no," these need to be addressed at the corporate level.

Questions to Ask

☐ *Do project teams have the resources (e.g., people, budget, equipment) and authority to implement their plans?*

☐ *Have the stakeholders made it clear what resources they are committing to the team and what authority each team members has? Do the stakeholders support changes or additional needs (or authority needed) throughout the work of the team?*

☐ *Does management work with functional heads in determining how to support cross-functional teams?*

☐ *Do cross-functional teams have the full support of functional heads?*

☐ *Is the functional work viewed by functional heads as of the same importance as team work, or as more or less important?*

☐ *Have the team leader and functional head negotiated about the functional resources they need and time length of the project?*

☐ *Have the team leader and the functional heads come to an understanding about the way they will assess the employees on the team from each function?*

- ❑ Are the lines of budgetary authority clear and supportive of team objectives?

- ❑ Do team members have the authority from their function to implement team objectives?

- ❑ Who has made it clear to the team members what authority team members have to represent and make decisions for their function?

- ❑ Are team leaders clear about the relationships between the team's work and the responsibilities of team members within their function?

- ❑ Are the functional heads of all the team members clear about and in agreement with the team leader about the relationships between the team's work and the responsibilities of team members outside the team (e.g., within their function)?

- ❑ Do management policies support a team-based culture with respect to providing the support team members need internal to the team? Has consideration been given to how much authority the team members are given, what resources are assigned to the projects, etc.?

- ❑ Do management policies support a team-based culture with respect to providing the team members the support they need external to the team re: authority, resources, administrative support, technology, and rewards?

- ❑ Are those who support the teams from outside the teams (administrative, purchasing, technical, etc.) included in team events and as necessary copied on team meeting updates or reports?

- ❑ What systems are in place to keep all the stakeholders informed?

- ❑ Has senior management had the opportunity to develop, review and approve organizational changes recommended to improve the focus on building a team-based organizational climate?

- ❑ Does senior management meet with team leaders on a regular basis to review operational issues? If the teams perform better when left alone for longer periods of time what criteria should be developed to determine what is meant by "regular basis"?

- ❑ Does senior management review plans for policy changes that affect the team with team leaders prior to these changes being announced to the employee population?

- ❑ Do team leaders regularly collect and report to senior management on team metrics including team process effectiveness, team performance and deliverables?

- ❑ Does senior management regularly review metrics around teams, including team process effectiveness, team performance and deliverables, and report to team leaders on the results?

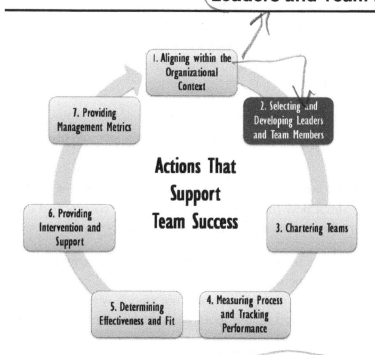

Actions That
Support
Team Success

1. Aligning within the Organizational Context

2. Selecting and Developing Leaders and Team Members

3. Chartering Teams

4. Measuring Process and Tracking Performance

5. Determining Effectiveness and Fit

6. Providing Intervention and Support

7. Providing Management Metrics

Effective team leaders and members are not born. They are developed, although they may have different capabilities at the outset. The most typical development opportunity team members and leaders get is from being assigned to work on or lead a team. When accompanied with direction and focus, on-the-job learning is a very valuable approach to development. Without direction and focus, there is a risk that bad habits may be acquired. Too many teams have members who bring old habits to new teams and influence inexperienced team members, thus spreading counterproductive behaviors.

When selecting team leaders, carefully assess their capabilities and the approaches they typical use. Too many "heroes" are seen as problem-solvers who can pull it all together at the last minute. Unfortunately, some of these leaders unconsciously create situations where the teams are not achieving or not working to plan so that the leader has to insert him/herself into the work of the team at the last minutes to "save the day." They may have created this scenario by withholding information they felt the team did not need to know, they may not have kept current with the team members' deliverables, or they may not have paid enough attention to whether or not the project milestones were on course. They also may not have worked to remove barriers for team members.

The ability to make it all come together at the last minute on the part of the leader initially seems like an important trait. However, if this is a typical style for the person being considered as a leader, more analysis needs to be done. The emphasis might be more effectively placed on helping that leader be more deliberate and more attentive to milestones or barriers.

Of course the unintended consequence of repeated selection of this kind of team leader sends the message throughout the organization that this kind of behavior is expected and desired.

If you talk with those team members who have worked under this kind of a leader, you will get an earful about how the behavior is demeaning. You may find that they mistrust senior leaders for allowing this kind of behavior to be recognized and rewarded.

Team members also can exhibit these traits, so assessment of capabilities and identification of development needs in the early stages of team member selection is important. Team members may "go it alone," not step in when other team members are having difficulties, and be shortsighted about what others may need from them.

Setting behavioral expectations early in the life of the team is critical for new and/or inexperienced team members to begin to learn effective team member behaviors. Interventions with the selected team leader prior to the team chartering meeting can help script what the team leader needs to express to the team members about his or her expectations.

Once the work has started, quick attention and communication about non-productive behavior on the part of both the leader and the team members helps reinforce what is expected by the organization. (See Establishing a Team Operating Agreement/Team Charter in Chapter 10 for more information about how to "start right.")

Depending on Experienced Leaders

A high tech company with many important projects taps an experienced leader to run a new product design project, even though the past project she ran has not quite been completed. Since she has successfully led four major projects in the past three years—more than any other team leader— the senior leaders believe that her selection ensures speed of project deliverables.

Impact on the Team

This team leader has not yet recovered from the last four projects and is burning out. This new assignment feels like a burden and has left her wondering if she is doing herself any favors by working so hard. In her current state of exhaustion, her ability to be an effective leader right now will be reduced.

When someone experienced is always chosen to lead interesting projects, young and as-yet-inexperienced "talent to watch" can become demotivated, feel less loyal to the company, and may begin looking for better opportunities. One key to look for is whether turnover is higher than expected for "talent to watch" since they see no opportunities to learn how to be a project lead.

These are typical mistakes made when creating project team structures:

- Selecting only seasoned team leaders.

- Assigning the "best and the brightest" to the project teams, always the same few people.

- Not capturing "lessons learned" at the end of a project.

- Not sharing "lessons learned" with the next project team members.

- Assigning inexperienced employees as team leaders without creating mentoring or other support systems to help them develop.

- Not measuring human process interactions on teams to find out which team members and team leaders are effective at team work.

Projects are excellent development opportunities. Companies may always choose experienced team leaders (for obvious and very good reasons). However, there are downsides to always using your experienced leaders. The message it sends to team leaders is mixed. On the plus side, they are valued. On the negative side, the company does not care enough to attend to their needs to refresh after strenuous projects. They may end up overworked due to their capabilities and become disillusioned with the company.

In some cases the unintended consequences of this may be that team leaders slow down so they are not always chosen. They may learn to not make it look so easy, and perhaps they may just meet deliverables or timetables so as not to always have to work so hard.

When companies take advantage of project team membership or team leadership as development opportunities, they create a win-win scenario. It is a win for the young talent when they are matched as co-leaders with experienced leaders. It is a win for team leaders who not only get support but also get an opportunity to mentor and develop (and maybe even learn something) from less experienced employees.

To take advantage of this opportunity:

- Identify young talent as a co-team leader who will develop leadership skills.

- Assign the experienced team leader as mentor.

- Make sure the developing team leader has specific leadership responsibilities within the team.

- Give someone outside the team (a learning coach for example) the responsibility to assess their progress and development. In some cases the team leader may not be forthcoming, may not give the learner valuable leading opportunities, may use the co-leader only to relieve them of administrative duties, etc. Someone outside the team needs to make sure the developing leader is learning valuable and appropriate lessons about leading teams.

The co-leadership model matches what the Center for Creative Leadership (CCL) recommends for development. Morgan McCall and his colleagues working at the CCL are usually credited with originating the 70:20:10 ratio. Allen Tough's research supported this position when he wrote in *The Adult's Learning Projects* that most learning occurs as part of the workflow and not in away-from-work training situations.

The 70:20:10 development model focuses mostly (70 percent) on learning through doing (on-the-job). Coaching and mentoring make up the next 20 percent, and 10 percent of learning occurs best in classroom training. The importance of this is that it extends the learning process well beyond the classroom or course paradigm and includes both workplace and social learning.

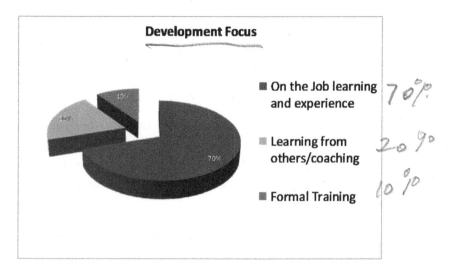

Development Focus

- On the Job learning and experience — 70%
- Learning from others/coaching — 20%
- Formal Training — 10%

Learning through experience alone is time consuming, expensive, and the results and outcomes achieved are hard to define or assess unless systems are in place for that purpose. Mentoring, development, and/or training processes provide a more systematic approach to learning. A combination of learning activities works best.

- It stands to reason that we retain information most effectively when it is learned in a practical context: learn by doing. This is most effective if the learner knows what he/she is expected to learn and someone is responsible to give feedback to the learner during and after the learning process.

- Learning is powerful when the lessons of experience are reinforced through informal discussion with people who have performed similar work. These veterans can point out common pitfalls, offer practical advice, and help steer the learner away from bad habits. Coaching and mentoring while learning through experience heightens and speeds the learning process.

- Learning is also effectively reinforced when it can be put to use quickly in the workplace.

- Training (classroom learning) is most valuable when it supplies technical skills, theories, and explanations that apply directly to what is learned through experience. It also is helpful when the topic needs to be learned quickly or when new behaviors need to be demonstrated or practiced.

- Learning is more effective when the value is expressed (for example, by the supervisor) and when what is learned is quickly integrated into the work environment.

To improve the effectiveness of development:

- The learner needs one-on-one meetings with his or her immediate manager to discuss how to apply the learning in his or her specific role.

- The learner's manager will have selected this learning specifically to support the employee (this is more likely in a hierarchical society), and/or the manager and learner will have agreed to this specific opportunity (the more participative approach). It is also helpful if the manager had similar previous experience.

- The manager rewards the learner for behavior change.

Formal project management training benefits both the new team members and those aspiring to be team leaders. It provides frameworks for how to manage and monitor team activities. It also focuses attention on how to stage the setup of teams and work with stakeholders to make sure there are proper lines of communication and work interactions are clarified.

Below is a set of questions to help the reader identify factors that set the stage for developing team leaders and team members.

Questions to Ask

☐ *Do project team leaders and members have previous experience? If not:*
- *How much do team members understand about what is expected of them as a representative of their function?*
- *Do they understand what they are to do and what is acceptable behavior when interacting with other team members?*
- *Are they partnered with someone, on the team or outside the team, who has experience and can coach or mentor them through the process?*
- *Is the opportunity of being a team member being framed as a development opportunity? If so, whoever is assessing their development needs to be mindful when they conduct performance reviews that people sometimes learn better or quicker from their mistakes.*
- *Have team leaders and team members with experience had the opportunity to share "lessons learned" especially with those who have less experience?*

☐ *Is training/learning/information made available as needed in the following areas:*
- *Leading teams*
- *Working on teams*
- *Influencing skills*
- *Conflict resolution/problem solving*
- *Project management*
- *Working in a multicultural team*
- *Leading/managing multicultural teams*

- *Using technology to support team communications*
- *Effective team communication protocols*
- *Understanding cultural differences*
- *Working on virtual or global teams*
- *Managing and leading projects across cultures*

☐ *Are employees able to access information from others who have previous experience in similar projects (e.g., using technology to access reports and lessons learned with either a Knowledge Management System or some other connecting device such as a list of email addresses or telephone numbers)?*

☐ *Do senior managers, even those who are not stakeholders, mentor leaders and team members?*

☐ *Are development expectations set at the beginning of the project and monitored throughout the project to assure learning is taking place?*

☐ *Are team project opportunities tied to development needs?*

☐ *Are functional heads involved in defining and communicating the development expectations?*

☐ *Are functional heads involved in measuring, assessing, and communicating their perspectives of the development progress to team members?*

An underlying cause of the success (or lack thereof) of global teams may reside in the definition of what it takes to be a good team member or leader. Cultural values play a significant role in these definitions. (See Chapters 13-20 for activities to help uncover and address cultural values and incorporate them into team protocols.)

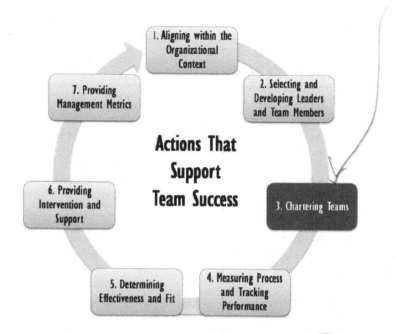

Actions That Support Team Success

1. Aligning within the Organizational Context
2. Selecting and Developing Leaders and Team Members
3. Chartering Teams
4. Measuring Process and Tracking Performance
5. Determining Effectiveness and Fit
6. Providing Intervention and Support
7. Providing Management Metrics

Setting the stage for chartering an effective team requires pre-work. Some companies require that a business case be built and presented to the senior leaders prior to the approval for funding the team's project. Other businesses or some projects do not require senior leader approval. Often when there is no senior leader approval, the upfront work and planning may not happen. This leads to lack of project clarity right at the beginning, a deficiency seldom compensated for during the life of the project.

Even if a business case is not required, decisions on a variety of topics are necessary in order to improve the likelihood of team success.

Preliminary Customer Acceptance Criteria (CAC) helps to identify who should be involved either as stakeholders and what functional capabilities are needed in the team members. This is true regardless of whether the customer is internal or external. For example, if a company wanted to install an Enterprise Resource Planning (ERP) system or centralize the accounting systems and reporting, that would impact internal customers.

To identify what capabilities are needed on the team, follow these steps:

1. Define (with the customer) the outcomes that are desired. Conduct a CAC analysis to clarity project scope and define nice to have vs. need to have. CAC are the standards required to satisfy the customer's order and expectations and gain the customer's acceptance of the final deliverables. A CAC analysis will tell you:

   - Who the primary stakeholder(s) is/are
   - What kinds of team member capabilities you need to include on the team
   - Who needs to play what roles to achieve the CAC and to assure team success.

   Then you can identify a preliminary list of:

   - Who might be appropriate team members
   - Who should approach the functional leader to ask for resources from their department/function and how they should do it
   - Who should invite team members to join the team and how the invitation should be done.

2. Now that the frame has been thought through, team members can be enlisted. How this is done can make or break a team. Are they assigned (Hierarchical Orientation) or made an offer/asked (Participative Orientation)?

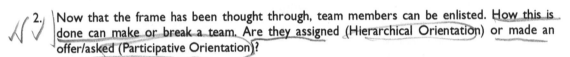

3. Once you have identified and enlisted the team members, focus again on additional stakeholders. Clearly the customers and the team members are stakeholders, but there are others that might be included on your list. For example:

   - Support staff
   - Members of functions that will be impacted either during the work of the team or by its outcomes
   - Purchasing, if you have to buy equipment or technology to be able to meet CAC.

Identification of resources needed (in addition to the functional expertise, such as software and equipment) helps start gathering data needed to create financial projections. Remember to include external resources such as equipment or software you need to purchase, vendors you need to include or inform, and customers or buyers. If well done, one might be able to provide preliminary Return On Investment (ROI) figures for the project before any significant amount has been allocated for the project budget and well before much of it is spent.

Analysis of who will be impacted by the project (including who is funding and/or championing it) helps develop a baseline list of stakeholders. Projects need champions (the major stakeholders) for whom the project has critical value. Any department that will be affected either by the outcome of the project or will provide resources to the team needs to be included in the list of stakeholders. All these people need to be considered in your communication and team updates. You can also:

- Conduct an initial estimate of how much time and effort the project will take
- Identify what needs to happen at the team chartering meeting, and
- Finalize who should attend the chartering meeting.

Conducting A Project Team Meeting

A global insurance company based in the US pulls together a project team of existing US process owners who are charged with the responsibility for transitioning their back office processing to an off-shoring entity in the Philippines. The intent was to save time and money by focusing the chartering meeting on the US process owners and what they need to do.

These process leaders convene in a team chartering meeting where they focus on which processes will be transitioned and in what order the transition will occur, and they leave the meeting with an action plan that they expect will take about seven months to achieve.

More than two years go by and, according to the process owners, less than two-thirds of the processes are completely transitioned. In their view, the employees in the Philippines have performance issues: they do not speak up, they come to meetings without any ideas on how to streamline processes, they accept that there are problems with customer calls but do not come up with ideas on how to meet customer needs without checking with the US process owners.

Impact on the Team

Since only the US members were invited to attend the team chartering meeting, those members of the team at the off-shoring facility were unclear about their role. No one at a high level in the organization introduced the employees in the Philippines to how the transitions would happen since each process owner took responsibility for their part of that transition. So the employees in the Philippines did not consider themselves part of a team—the team was the US process owners.

The employees in the Philippines were confused about their relationship with the process owners. Did they work for and report to the US process owners? Would the US process owners still be in charge once the process was transferred? Were the US process owners clients, leaders, or business partners?

These employees in the Philippines kept hearing that they were responsible to take over and "own" the processes once the transitions had occurred, but they kept getting mixed messages especially when the process owners stepped in and took responsibility to solve their problems. More confusion ensued from a lack of clarity about whether the US process owners' jobs would end once the transitions were complete.

Was the issue here that the process was not transitioned completely or that the soon-to-be-former process owners could not let go? How would the employees in the Philippines know when the process was theirs to own? Who was communicating this to both parties?

In the case above, the project took much longer than projected and incurred unexpected and unnecessary costs. This was due in part to not including the members of the Philippines team in the chartering and in a large part to cultural issues that we will explore in Part II of this book. The issues identified here include:

1. Organizational Issues – There was no clarity about the relationships of the group in the Philippines to the group of managers in the US. Were they customers, support staff, or partners?

2. Cultural Misunderstandings – The employees in the Philippines were unclear as to what was expected of them (this group had Hierarchical and Need for Certainty Orientations), while the managers were more Participative.

3. Performance Issues – The managers were not letting go even as they told their counterparts in the Philippines that they needed to own the process. This was due to the fact that once the process had been fully transitioned, their jobs would go away.

Not only should appropriate stakeholders be represented on the team, but they should take part in the first chartering meeting or team "kick-off." Several important outcomes of the first meeting include:

1. Most importantly, clarify the reason the team has been "commissioned" (mission/vision) and describe the importance of the outcomes to the organization and the customers (internal or external).

2. Having senior leader(s) attend, present, and/or open the meeting can focus sponsor and team member attention on the importance of the project to the organization. For people with a Hierarchical Orientation, this is important as it underlines the importance of the work.

3. Clarify all roles and responsibilities at the beginning of the project. This reduces the confusion as the project progresses. It clarifies for all parties what is expected of team members and outside sponsors as well. What the leader expects is important for those who have a strong Hierarchical Orientation. The clarity itself is helpful for those with a strong Need For Certainty.

4. Clarify as much as possible what individual team members are expected to deliver.

5. The best opportunity to get team members to work together effectively is to start the team project with some get-to-know-you opportunities. There will be more about this in the chapters on cultural nuances. This is important for relationship building, which is a precursor to building trust.

6. All team members need to have some authority to represent the stakeholders. Having worked this out with the functional leaders prior to the charter meeting can help all team members understand the roles each is to play.

7. Finally, invite appropriate stakeholders to attend the team charter meeting, and make sure they are represented on the team as well as being included in the stakeholder communication plan that the team develops.

Below is a set of questions to help the reader prepare for the team chartering meeting.

Questions to Ask

☐ *Who are all the stakeholders in this process/project?*

☐ *What departments are directly and indirectly affected by this work?*

☐ *What departments own the process and which are supportive to the process?*

☐ *Look at each stakeholder group. Does this stakeholder group need representation at all stages of the team's work? (For example, in the drug development process, research and development is early stage and regulatory compliance or marketing is later stage.)*

 • *If so, who should represent the stakeholder on the team and in what capacity will they be serving (support, decisions making, review of decisions made, reporting to the real stakeholder, etc.)?*

 • *If not, when do they need representation in the team? How much communication should they receive about the team's work prior to the stage at which their representative is joining the team? When they do need representation on the team, who should represent the stakeholder on the team, and in what capacity are they serving (support, decisions making, review of decisions made, reporting to the real stakeholder, etc.)?*

☐ *Do those chosen to participate in the team's activities have the full support of their functional head to do the team's work?*

☐ *What do they have the authority to decide?*

☐ *Do those chosen to participate in the team's activities understand the nature and breadth of the team's work?*

☐ *Do the team members understand the team's mission and know who the team's champion is?*

☐ *Is the team clear about its objectives—the expected outcomes and time tables for completion?*

☐ *Does the team understand how the team's work aligns with the company's strategic direction?*

☐ *Do the team members know each other and have an opportunity to get to know every team members' background, experience, strengths, and responsibilities toward this team's work?*

☐ *Are new members appropriately introduced to the team? This is especially critical when teams are cross-functional and have members who leave and enter the team at various times during the project.*

☐ *Is the team's success defined in ways that show its importance to the business? For example, in the process of developing pharmaceuticals, ending research of an unpromising compound should be seen as a success as it saves the company unnecessary expenses and allows focus on promising chemical compounds.*

☐ *Are the milestones clear and is some formal transition activity planned to move the team through the new phases beyond each milestone?*

☐ *Have communication protocols been established so that all team members know the following:*

- *Who gets which information and who gets copied?*
- *How will records be kept and by whom?*
- *What responsibility does each team member have for keeping these records?*
- *What responsibility does each team member have to inform those outside the team of the team's work?*
- *How quickly do team members agree to respond to requests from other team members?*
- *What medium is preferred by each team member (e.g., voice mail, email, etc.)?*
- *When does the team leader want to be involved (e.g., when barriers are identified, when snags occur, when things go faster than planned, etc.)?*

☐ *Do team members know where they can go for information (e.g., the team leader, an electronic bulletin board, etc.) on meeting schedules, to track progress of other team members, to access past reports, to access work schedules, etc.?*

Your team has attended the team chartering meeting. They have worked through the creation of the team's project plan. They have been working together for at least three months. How do you know how well they are working together, especially when team members are in different locations?

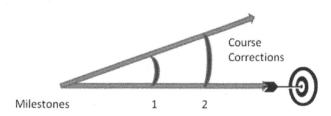

Many project teams use status update meetings to keep people informed and to make sure the work is progressing. In these meetings, progress is updated (and tracked), barriers are identified, the severity of the barriers or challenges is discussed, and mitigation plans are put into place with deadlines. This type of course correction meeting is important to keep the project deliverables on track.

Too often meeting attendees neglect to assess how the relationships are progressing – how well the team members are interacting (human process interactions on teams). Status updates focus on tasks and outcomes, process assessment (for example using questionnaires to measure how well the team members are interacting) provides equally important information. All sorts of behaviors (even really little things) can seriously erode trust and respect among team members. Look for questionnaires that assess such topics as conflict resolution, leadership, distribution of work, and communication. Here is an example of a situation where the team leader should suspect something is amiss and, perhaps conduct an assessment of how well team members are interacting.

Conducting Virtual Meetings

Jamal is holding a team meeting using teleconference. When they conduct status meetings there seems to be overlap in what members of the team are doing. *role definition*

Impact on the Team

The team leader is creating problems for himself by not attending to the concern that team members do not seem to be interacting with each other outside of team meetings. He has missed the sign that work is being duplicated due to a lack of communication between team members and that this is likely to create conflict, frustration, and rework.

If a team leader suspects that problems are developing between team members – evidenced by missed milestones and hand-offs between team members – he or she may call in an outside consultant to provide team building.

The activities used to build teams often seem like playing games. Senior teams and mission critical teams find they have no time (or interest) in this kind of "training." It feels like a "supply push" – I have this training program; it will help you. *true!*

Alternatively a team process assessment focuses team interventions, thus reducing the time needed to change and directing resources where they will do the most good (get the highest return on the investment). Rather than a "supply push," this feels more like a "demand pull" – the team responses point to and become the basis for a request to help develop those areas necessary for improvement.

The best assessments measure human process interactions and identify what is going well as well as what needs work. It is a bonus if the assessment instrument also measures whether cultural issues are creating barriers to the human process interactions on teams, and tracks improvement in interaction between team members over time.

Results of assessments are best if built into regular team meetings to provide a platform for team members to celebrate what they agree is going well and to talk about what they want changed. (See Chapter 22 for more information about instruments that measure human process interactions.)

Here is a task checklist with some of the factors that must be considered in defining the project deliverables.

Questions to Ask

❑ *What are the milestones for each segment of the project?*

❑ *What are the set/agreed upon timelines for each segment of the project?*

❑ *For each segment, what are the necessary steps/tasks to be undertaken to achieve the end point for this section/phase?*

❑ *Who is responsible for each task?*

❑ *Which of these tasks are dependent tasks and which are independent tasks? Independent variables are tasks that can be scheduled for completion almost anywhere within the general time frame for the phase. Dependent variables are those that need to be accomplished before the next task can be undertaken. (e.g., Determining what resources need ordering before placing the order. Placing the order is dependent on the identification of needed resources.)*

❑ *Are the dependent variable tasks clear to everyone? These are the tasks that will hold up a project or force it to extend time to complete the deliverables.*

❑ *How often are reports/updates expected and in what format?*

❑ *Is it clear who reports what to whom and when?*

❑ *Is it clear who is copied on the reports/updates?*

❑ *How often are meetings (or teleconferences or videoconferences) held to update everyone?*

❑ *Are communication protocols clear?*

❑ *Who has responsibility to frame the project budget? Is it the same person who has the authority to approve the budget? If not, does the team understand the difference?*

❑ *How are the expenses tracked? Who is responsible for tracking and reporting on them?*

❑ *If tasks fall behind, who has responsibility to approve the expenditure of more money (e.g., put more people on the tasks) in order to ensure deadlines are kept? Is this the same person who determines if the quality of the outcome can be lowered in order to keep the timetable?*

Here is a checklist with some of the factors that must be considered in setting the stage for team success regarding team human process interactions.

Human Process Interactions Notes

❑ *How are you, the team leader, or the sponsor, measuring human process interactions between team members?* often skipped

❑ *When new members are added, are objectives and progress responsibilities reviewed?*

❑ *What are the obstacles to effective communication (conflict resolution, trust, problem solving and communication), and how are these being measured?* yes!

❑ *Do team members feel this team membership is a developmental opportunity for them?*

❑ *Do you have ways of measuring critical team processes such as work distributions, clarity of roles and responsibilities, conflict levels, leadership, trust, etc.?*

❑ *Do you have ways of measuring whether there is improvement over time?*

❑ *Do you have ways to measure whether there are cultural factors that may become barriers to smooth team member interactions?*

✓

Example (and part of book?)

Here is a checklist with some of the factors that must be considered in setting the stage for team success regarding team communication and information sharing.

Technology and Communication Notes

❑ *Is there a technology platform that allows for project documents to be posted?*

❑ *Do all team members have access to the document repository?*

❑ *Do they all have the required level of proficiency to access this repository?*

❑ *Is training on the technologies offered to those who may want refreshers?*

❑ *Does everyone on the team have access to whatever communication technology is going to be used for the team meetings (conference calling, teleconference capabilities, video conferencing, etc.)?*

❑ *Do they all have the required level of proficiency to access and use this technology?*

Actions That Support Team Success

1. Aligning within the Organizational Context
2. Selecting and Developing Leaders and Team Members
3. Chartering Teams
4. Measuring Process and Tracking Performance
5. Determining Effectiveness and Fit
6. Providing Intervention and Support
7. Providing Management Metrics

When there is a disconnect between the culture of the team and the organizational practices, there could be problems. One example might be a Skunkworks team that adopts a working style quite different from the larger organization. "Skunkworks" is a term borrowed from Lockheed and typically refers to a small and loosely structured group of people who research and develop a project in secret for the sake of innovation. Skunkworks projects often are undertaken in secret with the understanding that if the development is successful then the product will be designed later according to the usual process.

On teams such as those, that are set apart from the rest of the organization, the team member and team leader style may not have to match that of the organization because of the formal isolation from the rest of the organization. Alternatively, the team might feel separate from the organization, more special, hence more cohesive. There might be a strong sense of being outsiders to the company, but "home" (an insider) within the team. Such teams might be more innovative because their thinking is different or unique from the typical way of thinking in the organization.

However, unless care is taken, when the leadership or team member style of regular teams does not match the competencies espoused by the organization, it is more likely that there will be tensions created between the team and the rest of the organization.

Team members may feel like the team's work is not connected to the work of the rest of the organization. Do the team members feel their work "fits" into the larger organization? If yes, what evidence of this "fit" do they have or look for? Do they feel they have the support from upper management? If no, what do they need and expect?

Serving Local Customers

In an effort to globalize, an American company acquires a company in Korea. The headquarters approach was a focus on "operational excellence." For Headquarters this meant no more special orders would be accepted. The Korean customers continued to expect the kind of customization they had received in the past from the acquired Korean company. The American leaders were not satisfied with the inability to acquire new customers or acquire larger orders from their existing Asian customers.

Impact on the Team

The approach of the Korean team before acquisition had been "customer intimacy" which meant they were willing to customize orders or take small orders and use that as an opportunity to develop strong customer relationships to establish their credibility and to increase the possibility of larger future projects. The Korean team lost face with their existing customers due to the executives' requirements for an operational excellence approach and therefore found it difficult to acquire new customers.

In the example above, the project outcomes are focused on the needs of a local customer. In this case the customer was in Asia, and the approach of the Asian division was to serve that customer according to local customs. These approaches were not aligned with how headquarters would have handled the business. This caused the senior executives to be dissatisfied with the Asian operations team.

In all these cases, and without intending to do so, barriers have been created. Senior leaders may pull away from or withdraw support from teams or team leaders whose approaches do not match (or whose approach to customer product development is not aligned with) the rest of the organization. In the case above, the difference in approaches caused an erosion of reputation, as well as a loss of customers, instead of the expansion that the senior team had planned.

Withdrawal of senior leader support creates barriers to successful deliverables of outcomes. Thus lack of support may negatively impact team members' reputations in the eyes of decision makers and may negatively impact team member career opportunities.

Too often what is really happening in the team is kept within the team, and outsiders make assumptions about what they think is happening. Communication with stakeholders is one key to preventing this lack of transparency from developing.

Making Mistakes – Upper Management

A research and development team at a pharmaceutical company has been working on identifying chemical compounds that they hope could be the next blockbuster drug for arthritis. They have been working together for over two and a half years and have had some promising results that have gotten to the efficacy stage. As they are due to report to the CEO on the status of their project, three things happen. 1) The company announces an acquisition of a former competitive company with a focus on Alzheimer's. 2) At the same time the company announces a hiring freeze due to this investment. 3) The CEO, who was supposed to address the R&D team at their upcoming global meeting on project status, now has demurred and will attend a meeting at the acquired company on that day instead.

Impact on the Team

The team members' are no longer sure of the corporate priorities. Does the company value the other projects more than theirs? Will their project funding be cut? Does this mean (some or all of) their funding will be transferred to the Alzheimer projects? Will they be transferred to different projects, or worse, lose their jobs? The concerns of the team members led to demotivation, a slowdown of productive work, and a reduction in team member collaboration.

On the following page, there is a checklist with some of the factors that must be considered in determining effectiveness and fit.

Questions to Ask

❑ *Do the team members feel their work "fits" into the larger organization?*

❑ *What evidence of this "fit" do they have or look for?*

❑ *Do they feel they have the support from upper management? If not, what do they need or expect?*

❑ *Do they get the opportunity to tell others outside the team how and what the team is doing? If others don't ask about the work of the team, can situations be created to provide the venue for team members to tell others about the work of the team (e.g., presentations or reports)?*

❑ *Do their functional area heads collaborate with the team and provide needed departmental support to ensure that the work of the team gets accomplished?*

Chapter 6
Offering Intervention and Support

Actions That Support Team Success

1. Aligning within the Organizational Context
2. Selecting and Developing Leaders and Team Members
3. Chartering Teams
4. Measuring Process and Tracking Performance
5. Determining Effectiveness and Fit
6. Providing Intervention and Support
7. Providing Management Metrics

Sometimes little things that could have been avoided create barriers on teams. Simple changes can do a lot to help team members understand their importance to the success of the team. Regularly measuring how the team members are doing and how well they are interacting helps identify developing problems before they negatively affect team outcomes. See Chapter 4 for more information on measuring human process interactions on teams.

This is especially valuable when improvement can be measured over time so that team members can observe how progress in team process influences team outcomes.

Intervention and support of teams over time depends on several factors including:

- Duration of the team charter

- Capability and performance of the team leader

- Criticality of the project timeline

61

- Nature of the objectives of the team (are others dependent on these outcomes?)

- Capability and performance of team members

- Factors external to the team (such as layoffs or other organizational changes)

- Human process interactions on the team—how well they work together and communicate with each other.

The key to providing support is assessing how well the team is progressing so as to keep current with the successes and barriers to success. Too often outside support is called in only when the team is already in deep crisis—for example, a crisis based on a loss of trust. Just like project milestones can tell the team leader whether the members are straying from the most efficient route to the target, process assessment provides early detection when interactions between team members start to go wrong.

Identifying Communication Problems

A virtual team leader called a team session to discuss the lack of trust on the team. She sent an email invitation. She was not using a standard email distribution list and was rushing to get the invitations out. She missed including two of the team members, and this was not the first time some team members had been inadvertently left off team communications.

Impact on the Team

This mistake caused at least two team members to completely lose trust in the leader and made others wary. Team members were routinely left off the communications who should have been included. This instilled fear that they not only were not valued on the team, but they also were afraid they were going to lose their jobs because there had been a recently announced reorganization and downsizing.

Here is a checklist with some of the factors that must be considered in providing intervention and support over time.

Questions to Ask

❑ *What is the level of experience of the team members and team leader with similar types of team projects? Do they need any type of support/training/mentoring to address any development gaps?*

yes!

❑ *Is progress in the communications, trust, and other process factors being measured so that timely intervention can refocus the team before too much time/energy/trust is lost?*

❑ *Are other interactions on teams (such as conflict and their resolution, work handoffs, rework issues and unclear or unresponsive communication) being tracked and reported out so that timely intervention can refocus the team before too much time/energy/trust is lost?*

❑ *Do your team measurements tell you what the team has identified as going well so that you can celebrate success with the team?*

❑ *Do your team measurements tell you what the team has identified as not going well and agree needs fixing so that you focus first on the low hanging fruit? Later you can work through as a team those areas where they disagree about what is going well or needs attention.*

❑ *Are team members notified when there are organizational or strategic shifts that could impact their work or the importance of it?*

❑ *Are support mechanisms available and ready when issues are raised?* yes. key pt.

❑ *Is the measurement done over time to track improvements and identify and communicate important changes?*

continuous assessment

Process metrics provided to senior leaders in an organization can supplement their outcome measurements. These provide a broader view of how well the company is progressing on its "mission critical" (those essential to the company's success) and other projects. Metrics also can help identify which teams and team leaders are most effective. In cases where there are several teams working on similar projects, such as pharmaceutical compound development teams, providing measurement data on how well the teams are progressing helps management make critical "go" or "no go" decisions earlier than if this information were not available. This has the potential to save what might otherwise be a considerable lost investment in both time and money.

While organizational practices may clearly define leadership competencies, the behaviors that are rewarded or allowed to persist present a clearer message about what is expected or allowable, or what is considered acceptable leadership behavior.

Depending on Difficult Team Leaders

There are several very experienced team leaders who are always tapped to lead important projects. For two of them, their projects succeed, but their team members often feel "used and abused" and former team members are reluctant to become members of their teams on future projects. Both during a project and after a project ends, there is unexpected turnover from within these teams.

Impact on the Team

Not reviewing the results of human process interactions on all teams leaves the corporation or organization with only "project outcomes and deliverables" on which to base their assessment of the leaders—too late to make important changes.

Comparisons of leaders' interactions with team members can provide people metrics to leaders of organizations to supplement their outcome measurements.

Measuring Impact by External Factors

A pharmaceutical client was measuring and comparing human process interactions on three compound development teams every quarter. The third assessment indicated that results from all three teams dropped dramatically. The assessment was conducted just after the company made an announcement that it was merging with one of its rivals.

Impact on the Team

The set of process assessments on the three teams showed how the merger caused both process and productivity to fall off as team members became more concerned with their own careers than with the work of the team. It took months to bring the team members back to a focus on the work of the team.

Senior managers who can track team progress (for example, measuring a baseline team assessment against change over time) and can compare the progress of the team or teams have several advantages:

1. If they can identify effective team leaders, they can:
   a. Leverage the leaders' skills thus assigning them to the most critical work.

    b.   Use skilled team leaders to mentor and develop newer team leaders.

2.   Leverage the resources of effective teams and/or team members.

3.   Identify development opportunities for newer team leaders and or team members.

4.   If they can measure team progress across several teams, they can:

    a.   Create early detection systems to address problems, barriers, and issues well before milestone are not met and deadlines slip.

    b.   Juggle needed resources and make these available only when needed, thus finding efficiencies in the use of certain resources.

5.   If they can measure team progress across the organization, they can monitor the impact of policy changes.

Part II

Internal Cultural Factors that Impact Team Success

The dramatic growth in global teams can become a time of great creative potential. In *The Medici Effect*, Frans Johanssen refers to the time of great creativity in 15th century Italy during the reign of the Medicis. He describes the Medici Effect as, "*...a time and place when different cultures, domains and disciplines stream together towards a single point...[which allows] for establishing concepts to clash and combine, ultimately forming a multitude of new, groundbreaking ideas.*"[3]

However, subtle cultural differences also bring with them a potential downside when team members and leaders fail to appreciate the affect that culture can have on member behavior. This section provides information on how to address the needs of various team members who bring different (and sometimes opposing) cultural values to their work.

The purpose is to help team leaders and team members develop cultural metacognition. This refers to a person's reflexive thinking about his or her cultural assumptions. According to Professor Roy Chua, "Cultural Metacognition seems to have a strong effect on how people effectively collaborate across cultures."[4]

Our cultural values are deeply embedded in our childhood and drive much of our behaviors and thoughts. Cultures define what is beautiful or ugly, dirty or clean, and what is considered acceptable or unacceptable behavior. We learn from institutions (religious affiliations, schools, family, communities, and other groups we may have joined) and from our environment (were we at war, in financial crisis, safe, well-fed, etc.).

What is considered effective leader and team member behavior is viewed through our cultural lens. Different cultural perspectives include but are not limited to the following:

- Definitions of what it means to "work together."

---

[3] Johannsson, Frans, The Medici Effect: What Can Elephants and Epidemics Teach Us About Innovation?, p2– Harvard Business School Press, 2006.

[4] Blanding, Michael, Cultural Disharmony Undermines Workplace Creativity, Harvard Business School Working Knowledge Magazine, 09 Dec 2013

- What is perceived as conflict vs. healthy interactions.

- How to handle conflict—maintain harmony or "be the squeaky wheel" and speak up.

- Decision making—should decisions be by consensus, discussed by the team members but decided by the leader, or just decided by the leader?

- Sharing of information—who gets to know what (need to know) vs. open sharing.

- Perspectives on what it takes to be an "effective" team leader or team member.

- Views on what confers status (and therefore who has more rights or power on the team). This can range from age, gender, education, salary level, title, and/or experience to proximity to headquarters for virtual teams. The influence of status itself varies by culture.

While many global teams use English as their language of business, this may put those who speak English as an acquired language at a distinct disadvantage. They will have to work harder to stay current with what is going on or what is being communicated. (Anyone who has tried to learn another language will know what I mean.) When you learn a language, you typically learn the first and perhaps the second dictionary meaning. Nuances of meaning are often lost, which potentially puts workers speaking an acquired language at a disadvantage.

Working in a second (or third) language is tiring work, and these team members may miss critical points. Also, those who acquire other languages may not be equally adept at speaking, reading, or writing the acquired language.

On the other hand, those with experience in more than one set of languages and cultures often have key insights into many aspects of how things are implemented in many different cultures. This implementation may differ from the implementation in the dominant business culture. This is confirmed by many research studies that indicate that multicultural teams, while sometimes a bit slower to reach goals, are often more creative in finding solutions than monocultural teams. This compensatory competency is crucial on multicultural and global teams and should be recognized both by team leaders and by management.

Handling Language Differences

The German member of an international team contradicts his team leader in team meetings, tells the boss he is wrong, and always answers first when the team leader asks for input. The team leader decides to change the team dynamics by asking the German to hold his ideas until after the meeting. After each meeting they go into his office and have long talks behind closed doors.

Impact on the Team

This scenario is filled with cultural overtones. The German way of communicating is to be direct, to point out errors in thinking, and to be clear and exact. This appears to most of the team colleagues (who come from a variety of European and Asian cultures) as rude and disrespectful to the boss. The boss is viewed as weak and ineffectual, and the German is viewed as not a team player. The after-meeting conversations in the boss' office also have unintended consequences. The rest of the team members think they are not valued since the leader spends so much time alone with the German…who has made it obvious to them that he disrespects the boss.

In this case, cross-cultural training for the team and coaching for the leader and the German member was the first step in smoothing team relationships. Coaching started with a focus on typical German communication styles (direct, desire for accuracy, tendency to use "upgraders" such as *always, must,* and *should*).

Team members discussed the impact of their different cultural approaches from the perspective of the unintended consequences of specific actions. They agreed to talk with each other when differences arose and to be open to learn more about differences.

Language and other cultural issues may confuse team members, cause a lack of trust, erode the leader's reputation, and may even unintentionally discriminate against some team members. Team leaders need to be cognizant of how to mitigate the negative impact language and culture might have on meetings, decision making, handling of conflict, dealing with time zone differences, and language differences.

This next part of the book will include information about strategies global team leaders and managers can use and aligns those strategies with particular cultural orientations. So briefed, team leaders can improve their approach to engaging and motivating all team members on culturally different and global teams.

For those with a Hierarchical Orientation, decisions need to be made, or approved, at the top. In some cultures, there is little or no discussion or involvement of team members in important team decisions. For those with a more Participative Orientation, this feels demeaning, as if their opinion is worthless. On the other hand, if a team leader with a Participative Orientation involves team members (with a more Hierarchical Orientation) in conversation when it is their expectation that an effective team leader makes decisions without input from the team, the team members may view the leader as ineffective and unable to make decisions.

Establishing New Team Leader Credibility

A British manager is promoted to run a team in France. In his first team meeting, he asks a lot of questions of the staff and tells them he will stop by their work space and talk to each one to find out what he/she is doing and to discuss work plans. Team members leave the meeting disappointed and distrusting of the new director. They talk among themselves about why he was promoted if he has to ask them what they do in their jobs.

Impact on the Team

While the director believed he was being inclusive (Participative Orientation), his new team felt he was not a strong, decisive leader. They expected and preferred him to be a leader with a more Hierarchical Orientation. They pointed to his participative behavior such as having to ask them what work they were doing and his coming to their work space instead of inviting them to his office. Because he did not start his leadership responsibility gaining the respect of the team, it took this leader over nine months and some cultural coaching to establish his credibility with his direct reports. During that time productivity lagged. With cultural coaching he was able to learn to be more directive and present a more Hierarchical Orientation in his behaviors which improved his ability to manage the team.

In some cultures meetings are formalities not places where issues are discussed or problems are raised. Instead, these are handled behind the scenes in social settings, such as drinks after work, and, because the alcohol "loosens the tongue," team members may be more likely to express their opinions. Team leaders who misinterpret or ignore these options for culturally appropriate approaches may limit their own effectiveness.

This chapter is focused on establishing leadership credibility for three scenarios:

1. New team leader to a new team (both start together).

2. New team leader who used to be a member of the team (promotion from within the team).

3. New team leader assigned to a team that has been working together under a different team leader.

NEW LEADERS WITH NEW TEAMS

If you have led teams before, you already know that team members on new teams are curious about the leader's background, capabilities, expertise, and leadership style. Regardless of what cultural background they come from, they will bring with them expectations about how they hope to be led (i.e., their perspective on the qualities and characteristics of an effective leader). You also have expectations on how you expect team members to behave. The expectations of what is considered effective behavior for a team leader or team member are based on the internal values of each person.

Members of remote teams may have opposing views on the qualities and characteristics of an effective leader, so you will need to lead depending on the situation and the people who will make up the team. Since both you and the team are starting out together on this new venture, this is the easiest situation in which to establish your credibility.

Of course, your personality and approach (a part of your cultural profile) should play a role, but being adaptive to team members' needs can make a difference as to whether the team functions smoothly, with unexpected bumps, or perhaps a continuous level of "noise" or dysfunction. Being a good and patient listener is one key to being an effective leader. Clarifying the team member expectations early in the team formation will prevent issues from cropping up later.

If productivity equals potential minus interference (Productivity = Potential - Interference) and cultural misunderstandings create interference, then cultural metacognition and understanding can improve business effectiveness.

Team members and leaders with an Individual Orientation are likely to be less interested in the leader's background than in how she or he conducts the meetings and manages the group. Those with a Group Orientation may be more interested in what they have in common with the leader and with others on the team.

Team members and leaders with a Hierarchical Orientation are more likely to want to know any information about their colleagues' background that might indicate status (such as their age). Those with a Hierarchical Orientation prefer a take-charge and decisive leader who can tell them what is needed. Those with a Participative Orientation want to be asked for their opinion, as well as be included and involved in problem-solving and decision-making. They are more likely to want to know how the leader will react to their input.

Team members and leaders with a Quality of Life Orientation are more likely to want to develop a collegial, cooperative relationship with their colleagues in order to promote team unity and focus. Those with an Achievement Orientation are more likely to be impressed by professional successes.

Those with a Need for Certainty prefer a high level of planning and structure on the team. Those with a Tolerance for Ambiguity prefer broad frameworks to rigid rules and requirements.

If one wants to be more effective, one needs to consider the benefits of adding flexibility and adaptability to one's preferred style. Please also note that recommendations that are linked to an orientation will be less effective for colleagues who have the opposite cultural orientation. Talking with the team about why these approaches are included helps develop cultural understanding on the team.

The tables below include recommendations with the cultural orientation for which this activity is most likely to be effective. While it is true that most team leaders and team members do not already know the cultural preferences of the others, think of these lists as a tool box of approaches to try in order to be culturally sensitive. If one approach does not work well, try another.

This is not meant as list of "must do." The recommended activities represent a list of suggestions that leaders can consider adopting depending on the make-up of the team, the leader's comfort level, and the business necessities. Leaders need to keep business necessities continually in their teams' view. Their challenge is to meld this with an effective cultural approach.

RECOMMENDED STRATEGIES FOR NEW LEADERS WITH NEW TEAMS

For those with **Individual and Achievement Orientations**:

- Share some of your background—focus on task achievement
    - Experience with teams including the number of years you spent on each team, leaders who were your mentors, and accomplishments and previous responsibilities on teams.
    - Describe some of the more difficult experiences you had and how you believe you would handle a similar situation on this team.

For those with **Quality of Life and Group Orientations**:

- Share some of your background—focus on relationship building
    - What you have learned that teams can do to be effective (build trust and relationship).
    - Allow them to submit personal questions to you in such a way as to provide anonymity.
    - Tell them things about yourself that they might find interesting (hobbies, favorite books or foods, etc.).

For those with **Hierarchical Orientation**:

- Have a senior leader introduce you as the new team leader.

- Ask the team to identify the qualities and characteristics of an effective team leader. Describe your strengths (and areas that need improvement). *yes how you learn what team orientations are*

For those with **Participative Orientation**:

- Make a commitment to grow and learn. Use their answers to frame your approach even if it is contrary to your preferred style of leadership.

For those with **Need for Certainty Orientation**:

- Provide a graphic such as a flow chart to show who the members are and what responsibilities they have in the team.

- Define the following and communicate them very clearly:
    - Who the project stakeholders are – and the involvement you expect them to have as stakeholders.
    - Team outcomes/customer requirements.

- Time frames for deliverables.

New Leaders Promoted from Within the Team

This is probably one of the more difficult leadership moves. You must be careful to establish quickly that you are the leader or others may not believe you were the right person selected for promotion. You also must be careful not to make any decisions (for example, about who does what) that might be perceived as either showing preference to certain team members or exactly the opposite—showing preference to others than those with whom you were most friendly.

Focus on the tasks to be accomplished, give feedback for achievements and performance challenges quickly and factually, communicate often, and explain your rationale to the team members (but do not be defensive).

You already know which qualities and characteristics of the previous team leader worked well for team members, and you might be wise to recognize and emulate these behaviors.

Establishing Leadership Credibility of a Former Team Member

The VP of Biostatistics and Clinical Programming for a global pharmaceutical company promoted a female employee from within the department. She was chosen to lead the team due to her excellent technical and people skills.

Impact on the Team

Her colleagues, a very large percentage of whom were first generation Chinese-American, did not understand why she was selected as she had less seniority than some of them and had less technical experience. This put her at a disadvantage immediately with her former colleagues.

This is a case where the potential for a Hierarchical Orientation among the majority of employees can provide an indication of what needs to be done to help to establish this leader's credibility. One organizational tactic is to give the new leader an even higher title to create more of the "power distance" between the leader and the former colleagues. This works well if the new leader is a bit younger than the other employees.

Another tactic is for a senior leader to make the announcement of this change in person to team. This gives the new leader the senior person's "blessing" as far as other colleagues are concerned. Senior leaders should take the opportunity of the announcement to stress the importance of both technological and people skills and to clarify company expectations for those from other cultures.

New team leaders promoted from within may have to contend with "taking charge" rather than "being friends" with former team mates.

RECOMMENDED STRATEGIES FOR NEW LEADERS PROMOTED FROM WITHIN THE TEAM

For those with **Need for Certainty Orientation**:

- Share some of your background—focus on educational background and degrees, mentors you worked with, and senior leaders who support you.

- Talk about what you have done in the past that has worked/past accomplishments.

- Share some of the experiences with teams you have participated on before.

- Define the following and communicate them very clearly:
    o Who the project stakeholders are and the involvement you expect them to have as stakeholders.
    o Team outcomes/customer requirements.
    o Time frames for deliverables.

For those with **Achievement Orientation**:

- Share some of the experiences with teams in which you participated that have been particularly successful.

For those with **Hierarchical Orientation**:

- Describe your strengths/status.

For those with **Participative Orientation**:

- Describe your areas that need improvement, aligned with their feedback about the previous team leader.

- Make a commitment to grow and learn. Use their answers to frame your approach even if it is contrary to your preferred style of leadership.

LEADERS INSERTED INTO EXISTING TEAMS

Leaders inserted into existing teams may have to contend with the attitudes about the previous team leader. This scenario is the most difficult in some ways because you may know little or nothing about the preferences for how the team members like to be led unless, of course, you are able to have a thorough debrief with the former team leader.

If the previous team leader was beloved (even if they were removed for performance reasons), taking their place will be particularly difficult as you may be seen as the "enemy." If you can, find out what the team members respected about that team leader, give credit to their positive attributes, and work to emulate them. If the previous leader was unpopular or perceived as incompetent, you would be wise to find out why. Getting a briefing by the former team leader, their supervisor, or project stakeholders may reveal important data. The primary stakeholder's perspective also could be very helpful.

If your style is markedly different from the previous leader's approaches, you will need to present your expectations early in the relationship so there are no surprises. See Part III for Activity Instructor Guides on how to conduct an intervention.

RECOMMENDED STRATEGIES FOR LEADERS INSERTED INTO EXISTING TEAMS

(Please also refer to the strategies for leaders in other situations, which can be found earlier in this chapter.)

For those with **Participative Orientation:**

- Ask the team to identify the qualities and characteristics of an effective team leader.

- Ask what qualities and characteristics of the previous team leader were especially effective with this team. Explain how your approach may differ, and why. (Do NOT make this conversation a gripe or glory session.)

NOTE: The fact that you "ask" (rather than "tell") makes this a participative approach. If you were to delegate the assignment and tell them to bring their ideas to the meeting, this would be appropriate for team members with a more Hierarchical Orientation.

SPECIFIC ASPECTS OF THE CULTURAL ORIENTATIONS NAMED IN THIS CHAPTER

Individualism Orientation	Hiring promotions should be based on skills
Achievement Orientation	Good manager should be assertive and decisive
Hierarchical Orientation	Work tasks are clearly presented; employees are expected to be told what to do
Quality of Life Orientation	Stress is on who you are, not so much on what you do (or have done)
Group Orientation	Relationships prevail over tasks
Need for Certainty Orientation	There is a belief in experts; there is a more formal and widely understood way of getting things done; there is comfort in structured situations; managers are expected to have the answers
Participative Orientation	Subordinates expect to be consulted; good ideas and suggestions can come from any organizational level

Specific Aspects of the Cultural Orientations Named in This Chapter

1	Individualism Orientation	Hiring promotions should be based on skills
2	Achievement Orientation	Good manager should be assertive and decisive
3	Hierarchical Orientation	Work tasks are clearly presented; employees are expected to be told what to do
4	Quality of Life Orientation	Stress is on who you are, not so much on what you do (or have done)
5	Group Orientation	Relationships prevail over tasks
6	Need for Certainty Orientation	There is a belief in experts; there is a more formal and widely understood way of getting things done; there is comfort in structured situations; managers are expected to have the answers
7	Participative Orientation	Subordinates expect to be consulted; good ideas and suggestions can come from any organizational level

LEADERS INSERTED INTO EXISTING TEAMS

Leaders inserted into existing teams may have to contend with the attitudes about the previous team leader. This scenario is the most difficult in some ways because you may know little or nothing about the preferences for how the team members like to be led unless, of course, you are able to have a thorough debrief with the former team leader.

If the previous team leader was beloved (even if they were removed for performance reasons), taking their place will be particularly difficult as you may be seen as the "enemy." If you can, find out what the team members respected about that team leader, give credit to their positive attributes, and work to emulate them. If the previous leader was unpopular or perceived as incompetent, you would be wise to find out why. Getting a briefing by the former team leader, their supervisor, or project stakeholders may reveal important data. The primary stakeholder's perspective also could be very helpful.

 yes!

If your style is markedly different from the previous leader's approaches, you will need to present your expectations early in the relationship so there are no surprises. See Part III for Activity Instructor Guides on how to conduct an intervention.

RECOMMENDED STRATEGIES FOR LEADERS INSERTED INTO EXISTING TEAMS

(Please also refer to the strategies for leaders in other situations, which can be found earlier in this chapter.)

For those with **Participative Orientation**:

yes — good way to start

- Ask the team to identify the qualities and characteristics of an effective team leader.

- Ask what qualities and characteristics of the previous team leader were especially effective with this team. Explain how your approach may differ, and why. (Do NOT make this conversation a gripe or glory session.)

NOTE: The fact that you "ask" (rather than "tell") makes this a participative approach. If you were to delegate the assignment and tell them to bring their ideas to the meeting, this would be appropriate for team members with a more Hierarchical Orientation.

Remote teams are more difficult to manage and lead than co-located teams. The most obvious reason is the lack of face-to-face meetings and informal conversations. Personal rapport can overcome difficulties that may be otherwise particularly difficult when virtual.

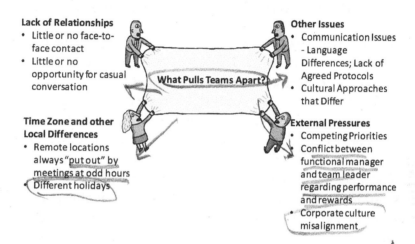

Lack of Relationships
- Little or no face-to-face contact
- Little or no opportunity for casual conversation

Time Zone and other Local Differences
- Remote locations always "put out" by meetings at odd hours
- Different holidays

What Pulls Teams Apart?

Other Issues
- Communication Issues
  - Language Differences; Lack of Agreed Protocols
- Cultural Approaches that Differ

External Pressures
- Competing Priorities
- Conflict between functional manager and team leader regarding performance and rewards
- Corporate culture misalignment

The more widely dispersed the team members, the greater the potential for stresses on the team. Too often people remotely are working:

- Virtually (in relationship-focused cultures, this makes being remote more difficult due to the lack of face-to-face contact during which they can build relationships with other team members).

- When they are most tired—during the evening or late night hours that are standard work hours for the team members at headquarters. It is precisely this time when they are at their least effective as thinkers and communicators. Late-night meetings for those not at headquarters can create the feeling that those required to be available for meetings at odd hours are somehow less valued members of the team (which could lead to morale issues). Time zone differences pull teams apart for reasons that should be obvious but often are not considered.

- In an acquired language, which makes it difficult for them to keep up even if they were not tired and had relationships with other team members.

Remote Relationships

Some cultures, such as Americans, Germans, and Australians (i.e., all of these are Individual and Achievement Orientation cultures), find it acceptable to form a group of people who have never worked together before and start a project with a focus on the tasks to be accomplished. In those cultures, prior relationships are not required for task accomplishment. People from other cultures, such as Latin American or many Asian cultures, may find it difficult to work with people with whom they have no relationship.

Building relationships remotely is very difficult. For more suggestions on how to build trust and relationships, see Chapter 12. The lack of face-to-face contact is exacerbated by the inability to have casual conversations in between team meetings. Without relationships, these conversations are not likely to happen. This is a double stress on the team because in many cultures, prior relationships would make it easier for team members to email or call each other for things outside of team meetings. Also, those who are remote do not have the luxury of asking questions when they see someone in the hall or at lunch. And when they do interact remotely, for example by email and telephone contact, those involved will miss the body language (all the facial expressions and hand gestures) and other nonverbal cues that carry so much of the message in any communication.

Improving Team Interactions

Maritza heard from a colleague that Greta was very hard to work with on a recent team project. She is so cautious when working with Greta that it seems to Greta that Maritza is avoiding her.

Impact on the Team

In her first couple of interactions with Greta, Maritza perceives that Greta seems to care most about the work and not so much about members of the team. This makes Maritza uncomfortable when she has to interact with Greta, so she tends to be quiet and withdrawn. Greta perceives Maritza as not being committed to the success of the team, so she "goes around" Maritza, leaving her out of some of the team interactions.

In the situation above, a focus on task (Greta's approach) versus relationship (Maritza's approach) has negatively impacted the work of the team. Maritza needs to know Greta better before she can trust her. For Greta to respond in effective ways with Maritza, she must understand how Maritza develops trust and how she communicates. In turn, Maritza would be helped in her communications with Greta if she understood that Greta's lack of personal communications with her does not imply either approval or disapproval.

RECOMMENDED STRATEGIES FOR REMOTE RELATIONSHIPS

For those with **Group Orientation**:

- Remember what others have said and follow-up. For example, with weather-related problems (tornado in the mid-west, monsoon in India, typhoon in the Philippines), with sports events (World Cup, Wimbledon), or with family events (birth of a child, marriages, etc.).

- Stay current on global news so you are aware of problems faced by your team members can understand the context in which they are working. You can ask questions such as, "I read that there was a typhoon in the Philippines. Are you and your family OK?"

- Encourage team members to contact each other and learn about each other's work, responsibilities, and outside interests.

NOTE: for both Group and Individual orientations, the level of disclosure and type of information shared will depend on topics that are culturally acceptable.

Lack of Relationships:

- Use photographs and include some personal information to help team members get to know each other. (See Part III for an activity to start the discussion about trust and relationship.)

Lack of Casual Face-to-Face Contact:

- Schedule face-to-face meetings periodically.

- Encourage including personal information by communicating things about your life such as "I am preparing for a five-mile bike race to support a charity," or "My son just turned five, and we'll have a party for him over this weekend."

- Use the concept of relationship-building conversation prompts or "ice breakers" to start meetings: "If an actor were to play you in a movie, who would it be and why?"

Technology Preference:

- Collect information about which technologies team members check first or most often. Share this with all team members so each knows how to reach others most quickly.

For those with <u>Tolerance for Ambiguity Orientation</u>:

- Whenever an important conversation takes place without all team members being present, make sure you share the conversation and decision or action that is an outcome of that conversation. (NOTE: This example relates to how the sharing of information is important.)

TIME ZONE DIFFERENCES

While some teams are co-located and made up of team members from various cultures, most global teams are virtual. Many companies are moving to a 24/7 service arrangement where they have people at work around the globe at all times and want the work to travel from one work group to another so work is always in progress.

The belief is that this will speed up the work and mitigate the time zone differences. Technically, assuming their teams are aligned in work streams that can rotate the work smoothly from one time zone to the next, this is feasible. Call center coverage is a good example of this. There can be call centers open 24/7 so that customers who live anywhere can be served.

With IT teams (especially for tightly integrated activities such as development projects) and projects having more specialized responsibilities, 24/7 handoffs are not feasible. Handoffs are often utilized for IT support of tech bugs (such as service requests), but there is almost always a loss of efficiency.

Time zone differences put pressure on virtual team members, especially when the language of business is not their first language. Too often meetings are held during the office hours of headquarters and late at night in countries half way around the world. After a long day at work, these team members, who are already tired, are required to stay up late and work in a less-familiar language.

We often forget that our team members are in different times of the day (or night) when we have meetings (teleconference calls, for example). Unless we pay attention to this, we can undermine the sense of fairness on the team. It may seem to those who are remote that some team members (those who are not remote) are favored.

Pulling the Team Apart

Ahmal, the project manager in India, is holding his project team meetings at 9:30 AM Mondays in order to start the week with an action plan. This is quite inconvenient even for his Indian colleagues in Mumbai. They often have difficulties being there on time for the meeting due to the unpredictable traffic in Mumbai.

Impact on the Team

Some of his team members in other countries who also are on the call do not speak up and often seem distracted. Ahmal's virtual colleagues believe that he does not really value their opinions or contributions.

In Germany the scheduled meeting time is 6 AM.

In Korea and Japan, it is 1 PM. *more like it!*

In some parts of the US the scheduled meeting time is midnight Sunday evening/Monday morning, and in Buenos Aires it is 1 AM Monday morning.

Many of his team members are exhausted because they are on the meeting call at very difficult time slots for them and their families.

More and more companies have true global teams with representation from many continents. Teams that are European and American, American and Asian, or Asian and European have fewer time zone challenges. So when one is setting up team membership and establishing regular meeting times, extra thought should be given to the locations of prospective team members.

If not, impressions may include:

- Extra work hours are expected of others but not those at HQ.

- The work and opinions of others are less valued because there is no recognition of whether or not the people in other time zones might be tired from having already worked a full day.

- It is disrespectful in some cultures to expect people to cut into family time to conduct work (Achievement vs. Quality of Life Orientation).

To compensate, global team leaders may choose to stagger the start time of team meetings so that all members are equally "put out" over the course of the project. This often minimizes the unintended consequences of disillusioning remote team members. It recognizes that those working in acquired languages need to be at their freshest when they are working on difficult challenges.

Other local differences also create stresses on the team.

1. National holidays vary. If team leaders are not aware of the holidays celebrated by their team members, they might call meetings that interfere with religious or other holidays. Holidays or local customs about time off may impact response times. Team members may feel that they are being treated with disrespect when others do not know the holidays or other local customers regarding work attendance.

2. In strongly Group-Oriented cultures, family events such as the baptism of children (the Philippines) or visiting parents during the traditional New Year or on holidays to honor the dead (Asian cultures), can create pressures on team members if their families expect attendance at these events and work requires otherwise.

Here are some strategies for each of the negative forces that can pull remote teams apart or diminish their effectiveness. The related cultural orientation is also listed. Strategies for strengthening the forces that draw remote teams together also are provided.

Please note that the suggestions offered that are appropriate for one cultural orientation may annoy those who have the opposite orientation. Effective team members talk about why they are conducting activities so that all team members understand the cultural differences. Team leaders need also to attend to the needs of all team members of all orientations.

Team development maturation comes when team members understand why different approaches are taken and groups on either side of the continuum of a particular orientation feel heard and understood.

RECOMMENDED STRATEGIES FOR TIME ZONE DIFFERENCES

For those with Need for Certainty Orientation:

- Send out meeting announcements well in advance of the meeting.

For those with Quality of Life Orientation:

- In meeting announcements, include the time zone start times for all attendees.

- If possible, rotate the meeting times so that everyone is equally "put out" by having to work outside their regular office hours. Schedule teleconferences at varied times on a 24 hour schedule. (On global calls, someone is going to be working at night. Make sure it is not always those who are remote or those for whom English is an acquired language.)

Other Local Differences:

- Send out an annual holiday list.

- Have a conversation about what the local customs are regarding taking time off for a holiday. For example, some countries typically take an extra half a day off before a holiday.

- Ask questions about the festivities for these holidays; after the events ask if anyone wants to share what they did that was special for the holiday.

For those with Group Orientation:

- Start every meeting by asking people to introduce themselves and announce the time of day in their current location (builds relationship).

Handling Local Family Events

Manuel works in a call center team in Manila, and he has been invited to attend his nephew's baptism. Manuel asks for three days off to go to the baptism, which is being held on another island in the Philippines. His team leader refuses the request.

Impact on the Team

Manuel resigns because family is more important than work in the Philippines, and the rest of the team loses respect for the team leader. The team leader is not seen as sympathetic to the geographic issues about travel between islands in the Philippines. Nor does he seem to understand the importance of attendance at family religious events.

Local understanding and flexibility can make a significant difference in the attitudes of the team members.

If the team leader goes out of his or her way to allow what may seem to others to be an unusually long request for time off, in the Philippines there is an expectation that Manuel now "owes" the team leader. There is a recognition that the leader did something special and "took care of" Manuel in return for Manuel's loyalty (Hierarchical Orientation). This may result in a more highly committed team member who will work harder to please and pay back what is owed to the team leader. However, it can be made clear by the team leader that he expects the lost work to be made up. This can be done subtly without making the understanding seem like a demand.

PRESSURE TO PURSUE LOCAL PRIORITIES

Cultural differences, local customs, organizational structures, funding and budgetary requirements, and other factors external to the team may create tensions and pressure to do outside work that would diminish the work of the team.

If the team leader is at a lower employment level than the functional supervisor of a team member, those with a Hierarchical Orientation may respond more quickly and more fully, or first to the person with the higher title. In some cultures they may respond first to someone who is part of their in-group (Group Orientation), to someone who is the same gender, or to someone who is older or of a higher status (Hierarchical Orientation).

As we saw in the first part of the book, there are many organizational factors that put pressures on team members. Often this distracts from the focus team members need to have to accomplish their deliverables.

Scheduling Resources

Helen, who is the operations specialist on the team, has been called to the manufacturing floor by her manager to troubleshoot a problem that has occurred just prior to a visit from a prospective customer. She misses an important virtual status meeting with an existing customer, and her team members need to cover for her.

Impact on the Team

Team members feel insecure when giving a status update on Helen's specialty. They feel that she has let them and the customer down. They also feel that Helen was weak because she did not negotiate with her manager to prevent this unfortunate double scheduling.

Who has priority? Typically it is whoever has to respond to customer needs. In this case, there was an existing customer and a prospective customer. Who should get priority is a difficult decision to make. If they had asked themselves how they could have Helen at both meetings (both/and vs. either/or), they might have found a way to work out a more reasonable customer schedule that would not have put Helen in this difficult position.

External communication with stakeholders (for example, Helen's manager) can avoid double booking especially when customers are concerned. In this case if the manager and the team leader had established a relationship and an understanding about both of their needs for Helen's expertise, they might have avoided the negative impact on the team. This also puts special pressure on Helen to communicate the problem to both of her supervisors (which requires comfort with a Participative Orientation).

RECOMMENDED STRATEGIES FOR PRESSURE TO PURSUE LOCAL PRIORITIES

For those with <u>Tolerance for Ambiguity Orientation</u>:

- Recognize local, functional, and team priorities and differences. Create a time in your meetings for the sharing of barriers to completion.

For those with <u>Hierarchical Orientation</u>:

- Use your influential (who you know) and positional power (title) as a team leader to get relief for your team members.

- Intervene with functional leaders to get support for the team members that they supervise.

For those with <u>Need for Certainty Orientation</u>:

- Provide information to functional leaders on the responsibilities and accomplishments of their supervisees who are on your team.

- Communicate with internal stakeholders to keep them informed of schedules, especially blocked dates and times. The use of group calendars works well (also for those with a Hierarchical Orientation).

COMMUNICATION

LANGUAGE DIFFERENCES

Anyone who has worked to acquire a second language knows that nuances are often missed. Some cultures liberally use metaphors and acronyms (Americans are well-known for their use of sports metaphors) that do not translate well.

Handling Language Difference

The US Director Scott asked for the project status report to be "submitted ASAP." He waited and waited and did not get the final report from his Asian Analyst, Leona. Leona understood "as soon as possible" by its literal translation, meaning that she could get around to submitting the final report when it was possible after her other work was complete.

Impact on the Team

Scott sees Leona as a slacker, and Leona sees Scott as being unfair and not a good communicator. She thinks he is demanding something now that is different from what he told her earlier.

---

good example

Since the literal translation of "as soon as possible" does not mean "do it now," both Leona and Scott have negative misperceptions of each other. Even if both speak the same language, words and phrases may mean different things.

Leaders also need to remember that many who have acquired English as a second language learned British English, not American English.

also true

LACK OF AGREED PROTOCOLS

> ### Building Relationships
>
> Jayden has heard from several of his team members that Alec, the marketing subject matter expert, does not respond to team member requests quickly, gives only the basic information that was requested, and does not give any context. This is making it difficult for others to work with him. Jayden holds a performance conversation with Alec.
>
> ### Impact on the Team
>
> Alec now distrusts his team members. He feels he has been efficient and had responded as quickly as he could, given their requests. Since they all have been on the team the same amount of time he has been, he expects them to have kept up with content and context, which is why he makes his replies succinct and to the point. He is now disillusioned with the team members and the team leader.

There could be several reasons why Alec responds in this manner.

1. Alec may have an Individual Orientation and expects others to find what they need to know about context themselves. He may feel that he takes care of keeping up on the documentation in the electronic repository, so why can't others?

2. It could be that Alec responds quicker when he receives requests using his preferred technology. If he prefers telephone and others use email to try to get his attention, he may not respond as quickly when email is used. It would help if everyone knew what the team members' technology preferences were and used the one that Alec is likely to respond to most quickly.

3. It could be that a protocol needs to be developed to agree on what is meant by a "reasonable response time" and to define what communication is expected if that time frame cannot be met.

4. People with a Need for Certainty expect and prefer more detail (background, context and explanation), and it could be that Alec does not have this orientation and does not understand the needs of other team mates.

EQUAL ACCESS TO TECHNOLOGY

Does Alec work remotely in a home office and therefore does not have access to high speed internet or the capability to hold conference calls? Organizations often disadvantage employees in locations where there are few employees by not allowing them the same access to technology that the larger offices enjoy.

While Alec may be responding as quickly as he can, it may not be entirely his fault that he cannot respond as quickly as other team members. There are countries where the infrastructure reliability is spotty. Are we holding Alec to a standard that is unreasonable due to his location and access to technology?

If a team leader and team members understand the challenges of all team members, there is a higher likelihood that issues such as perceived slow response times will be compensated for as well as tolerated.

Assuring that all team members have access to technology also includes making sure they can access the meeting documentation and reports from some electronic repository. This means that team members need to be held accountable to make sure the documentation is posted and posted in a timely manner for everyone to access, especially those who are remote. They also need to be held accountable to review the documentation and keep current on content, decisions, changes in priorities, and action planning tasks and responsibilities.

DIFFERENT CULTURAL APPROACHES

In the situation above, Alec may feel he is being efficient by giving basic answers. In high context cultures, people often understand much deeper meaning than is actually spoken or written. In low context cultures, more is spelled out in the verbal communication.

NOTE: Attitudes about time also differ from culture to culture. Monochronic cultures (cultures in which people like to do just one thing at a time) have a sense that there is an appropriate time and place for everything. They do not value interruptions and hold that if something is important enough, then time frames can expand to make sure that the proper attention is given to the task. Polychronic cultures like to do multiple things at the same time, manage interruptions well, and have a willingness to change plans.

If Alec is not responding quickly enough, perhaps a conversation with the team about what is an acceptable turnaround time and the barriers some team members face (for example with technology or time zones) might help them come to a better understanding or agreement.

RECOMMENDED STRATEGIES FOR COMMUNICATION

General Comments:

- Restate complex ideas in simple language. Paraphrase important points to help those who speak an acquired language.

- When on teleconferences, ask each speaker to say his/her name before they speak.

- Explain acronyms and other statements that you want all team members to understand (metaphors, analogies, etc.). Create a list of definitions especially for technical terms and acronyms.

- Acknowledge that communication is more difficult on remote teams. *yes, state the obvious!*

For those with **Achievement Orientation**:

- Establish the importance of time by clarifying the time commitments expected and holding people to these commitments.

For those with **Individual/Group Orientation**:

- Understand that the willingness to disagree, differ, and discuss may vary. ✓

- Recognize the cross-cultural difference including the amount of clarity and context preferred in communication. High context cultures (Group Orientation) are more likely to need less context than those from low context cultures (Individual Orientation).

NOTE: Individual or Group Orientation will impact the position they take (disagreement for Individual vs. harmony for Group).

For those with **Tolerance for Ambiguity Orientation**:

- *yes* Realize that thinking processes may differ (convergent vs. divergent thinking). Talk about it and value both approaches by encouraging them equally.

For those with **Hierarchical Orientation**:

 ✓ - Recognize that the expectations of leader responsibilities may differ. Help team members understand differences between perspectives. Manage their expectations.

For those with **Quality of Life Orientation**:

- Make known about the technology challenges team members might be facing to increase understanding among team members.

Other activities to consider:

- Understand that for those working in an acquired language, there is more likelihood for misinterpretation. Ask more clarifying questions and encourage others to do the same. Listen for potential misinterpretation.

- Acknowledge that accents may be more difficult to understand. Ask everyone to speak slowly.

- Provide visual materials for attendees to prepare from and follow. Use graphics as often as possible.

- Paint "word pictures." Describe what things look like and describe how things work starting with something they already know (e.g., a debit card is just like a credit card except...).

FORCES THAT PULL REMOTE TEAMS TOGETHER

The news is not all bad. There are also forces that pull teams together. Team members and team leaders who understand the forces that pull teams apart know that they must attend to those issues as well as using the techniques and tactics that help pull teams together.

Forces that Pull Teams Together

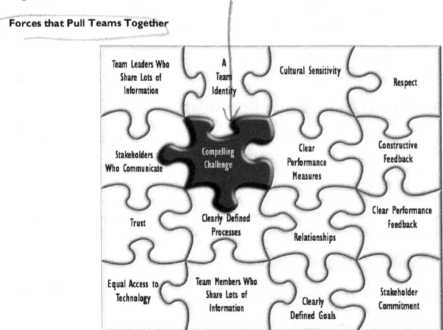

Creating a Compelling Challenge

WXY company wanted to alter their manufacturing process to add color to their product. This was seen as an insurmountable task that no one had yet figured out how to make happen and still maintain a reasonable profit margin. A cross-functional action learning team was created with members from finance, marketing, product R&D, manufacturing operations, the union, and the supply chain. Each member had been identified as "talent to watch," and they were tasked with studying the problem and making recommendations to the senior leaders.

Impact on the Team

The team members were thrilled to be selected for so important a project. They were honored that the senior executives felt that they were specialized enough to find and recommend a solution. They took seriously their responsibility to develop their expertise in areas other than their functional areas.

With this client, the challenge was very compelling. The problem selected was one that had never been "cracked," and those asked to work through all the options and issues and make recommendations made this opportunity desirable. When the team made their recommendations to senior management, they were promoted into new responsibilities and tasked with the challenge to "make it happen."

Not all projects are as compelling. Not all teams are able to work together effectively and find they have no difficulties relating to each other along the way. Sometimes cross-functional boundaries (think R&D and marketing) are just as difficult to cross as cultural boundaries. It helps to remember that culture is not the only driver of workplace behaviors.

As you can see from the graphic below, people bring their personal background, history, and personality into the workplace. There are environmental factors, such as regulation in the pharmaceutical and finance industries or governmental stability that may impact workplace behaviors. Internal organizational practices may direct employees to behave in certain ways, and of course the national values that one brings will also impact how one behaves at work. What tends to happen is that cultural values are rarely considered as factors that drive workplace behaviors.

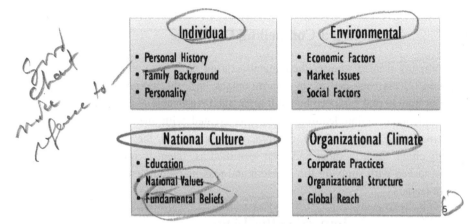

Organizational or corporate expectations, when added to the cultural complexities, indicate that training is not always the answer. Yet companies still expect that a half or full day of training will "fix" what is wrong with teams. This attitude in itself is a Short-Term Orientation response: fix it quick, put a Band-Aid on it, and check the box that we "did something."

The attitude about teams is based in cultural values. Group-oriented cultures view teams from an in-group or out-group mentality. Individualist cultures view teams as independent workers coming together to work on a project in their own individual ways, bringing their individual capabilities to the team. This is often why team building is more necessary in some Western (and more individualistic) countries. In some Asian countries, when there is a problem on the team, the leader is simply replaced. The expectation is that the team leader is in charge and responsible to make it work (Hierarchical Orientation). If the leader cannot fix the problem, then he/she needs to be replaced.

A deeper analysis of the causes of the problem is highly recommended before offering any training. The areas to consider include the following:

- Organizational Design Issues – Is there something about the way the group is organized, or how the people are titled, or about the performance measures that may contribute to the problem? For example, company GGG in Korea promotes a young, well-educated employee to supervise more experienced and older employees. Due to the Hierarchical Orientation, the younger manager might not be respected because of his age. To make up for the age disparity, the organization gave the younger employee a title two levels higher than his staff.

---

5 Sourced from various published articles authored by John W. Bing Ed.D © John Bing 2000 - 2014

- Performance Issues – Sometimes there are team members who actually are not pulling their weight and others know it. For example, Company CCC has one manager responsible for work on the manufacturing plant floor who, in a previous job, was also a manager (Hierarchical Orientation) but not a "working manager" (Participative Orientation) – someone who had specific functional responsibilities in addition to his/her management duties. Because of that, he is less comfortable getting his hands dirty, even when things go wrong, or stepping in to help. He avoids this kind of work. His colleagues wonder why he is not being held accountable by senior management to do what is expected of him.

- Cultural Issues – These can be expectations of team members about the qualities or characteristics of an effective team leader. For example, some team members believe it is effective for leaders to tell them what to do. This may especially be true of those with strong Power Distance preferences (Hierarchical Orientation). Some team members may prefer to receive strong and clear directions (those with a strong Need for Certainty). Others (for example, those who may have a preference for Participative Orientation and a Tolerance for Ambiguity) may view these kinds of leader as micromanagers. They prefer to be given the outcomes required and some parameters. They think that an effective leader talks through how to approach the outcomes and allows questions and ideas for discussion (Participative Orientation).

It's important that team leaders think through the likely causes of team problems. When the differences are cultural, they can cause all sorts of misunderstood actions between team members. Let's take this one step further and look at these behaviors from the leader's perspective. A leader who believes strong direction is best may view those who prefer other approaches to be:

- Uncommitted to the team when they challenge the status quo or ask questions to uncover issues.

- Disrespectful because they challenge the leader, or come up with different approaches, disregarding what the leader has delegated.

- Unwilling to get the work done, instead wasting time when the leader has made it clear what is to be done.

The opposite scenario is not any better. A leader with a more participative approach sets general goals and lets the team members figure out how to meet those goals. This leader may resent those team members who prefer more explicit direction and assume them to be:

- Lazy.

- Unable to think for themselves.

- Time wasters because they wait for the leader to give explicit instructions before they can begin work.

While a training needs analysis can uncover some of the cultural problems, more of a consultative approach to uncover root causes or drivers may resolve the problems. If not, a cross-cultural training course, based on the needs analysis findings, will offer more targeted solutions. (See Part I for questions to ask.)

CREATE A COMPELLING CHALLENGE

Sometimes companies have difficulty acquiring and retaining remote talent. Some cultures have a Hierarchical Orientation, and potential employees in those countries may prefer to be hired by companies with strong brand identification to achieve a level of status connected with that strong brand.

These employees may also prefer to be on a recognizable or branded team, as this confers status. Team leaders can brand their teams with names, slogans, clothing, or a look for all communications. Employees from Group-oriented cultures often find this sense of belonging attractive.

Creating an Organizational Culture of Compelling Challenges

Juana's team worked very hard creating a new product line for their consumer products division. The run-up costs were high, and it was quite some time before the company made a positive return on its investment. Juana kept her team informed of financial progress even after the team had disbanded.

Impact on the Team

Members of the team renewed their camaraderie every time Juana sent an update on the sales figures. They held a celebration once the breakeven point was reached. This got the team members personally invested in the company financials because they were kept informed of the value their product brought to the company.

Another approach to creating a compelling challenge is to link the work of the team to the success of the corporation or to the corporate strategy. Having high-level stakeholders who formally promote team goals can create a compelling challenge, especially in high Power Distance cultures. It may surprise some team leaders that employees often work better when they know why they are doing something. Answering that question can create a compelling challenge.

It's important for the principal C-level leader to inform the team how the work of the team relates to corporate strategy. If the team's outcomes are "mission critical" (essential to the growth or continued existence of the company or division), this information can increase the team's motivation to accomplish its goals, especially if they know their work is supported at the highest levels in the organization. Conversely, if team members believe that their work is ignored at the highest levels in the organization, it can demotivate the entire team.

Effective leaders also help their teams understand the financial implications of the work of the team during the various stages of achievement of team milestones. Team members find it useful to know:

1. What does it cost for the team to work on the project?

2. How else has the company invested in addition to the cost of the team members (software, equipment, supplies, etc.)?

3. If the team misses deadlines, what does this do to the return on investment calculation (i.e., how much longer will it be before the company begins making a profit)?

4. What is the expected return on investment to the company after this project is completed?

5. How long will it take to pay for the investment of time and materials before the profit is realized?

Such information helps team members understand the importance of the project to the company strategy, to its financial health, and to achieving the project outcomes on time and under budget.

Giving the employees an entrepreneurial perspective can make a difference in how employees set their priorities and work to accomplish deliverables. Many companies do not share deep financial details with their employees and just expect the employees to take their word that the work is important to their strategic plan. Very few employees can talk specifically about how their work contributes to the bottom line of the business. Not many understand how important cash flow is.

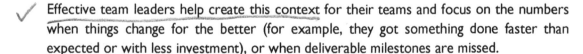

Effective team leaders help create this context for their teams and focus on the numbers when things change for the better (for example, they got something done faster than expected or with less investment), or when deliverable milestones are missed.

Aligning with Corporate Strategy

From Wiler's perspective his team seemed to be dragging their feet. The project team had been working together for several years to create a new financial software package for their clients. No matter how much he tried to impress upon them that the Statement of Work had some hard deadlines coming up soon and that he was concerned that they were going to slip these deadlines, it seemed to make little or no difference in the concern of the team members about meeting these deadlines.

Impact on the Team

Wiler had neglected to share with the team the financial overview of this project and the financial penalties for late deliverables. The team viewed his insistence as a lack of respect for the hard work they had already put into the project. The harder he pushed, the more it annoyed them.

RECOMMENDED STRATEGIES TO CREATE A COMPELLING CHALLENGE

For those with <u>Need for Certainty Orientation</u>:

- Share information about how and what your team is working towards is important to the business strategy.

- Hold a project or team chartering face-to-face or through video conference for the purpose of setting protocols and defining the challenge/purpose/mission of the team.

- Clarify the objectives of the team and work with the team members to determine how they can be achieved under time and resource limitations.

- Confirm understanding of the goal(s) for all team members. (Also works for Group Orientation.)

For those with <u>Achievement Orientation</u>:

- Holding team members accountable to achieve the goal(s).

For those with <u>Individual Orientation</u>:

- Explain why efficiency and effectiveness are important (i.e., the cost of holding meetings).

INFORMATION SHARING

One of the aspects of the Need for Certainty Orientation is that information **held** is power. The converse of that is the Tolerance for Ambiguity Orientation (the opposite end of that dimension) in which information **shared** is power.

Sharing Information

Sandy and Chad walk out of the triage meeting together. In their one-on-one conversation, Sandy delegates a task to Chad that had been discussed in the meeting.

Impact on the Team

Two other team members who were unclear about who was going to handle the task took it upon themselves to resolve the issue and were dismayed at the next meeting to find that they had been duplicating the work assigned to Chad.

Too often decisions get made and not communicated to all the team members. This is a special problem for all those who do not work in the location of the team leader. Hallway, cafeteria, and water cooler conversations often go undocumented, and while work may get done, it is also possible that work is either duplicated or dropped since no one is held accountable. Handoffs also need to be carefully orchestrated, especially if work is delegated or handed downstream virtually. Misunderstandings occur on deliverables, and expectations on time frames may be unreasonable due to local customs or infrastructure issues.

Cross-cultural and virtual team leaders and team members need to take special care to document and post so everyone can access the information and to have deeper discussions about what is expected in terms of timing and outcomes.

This may be uncomfortable for leaders who prefer a Participative approach to managing their teams. Rather than asking the team members if they understand—because the answer is almost always yes—it is more effective to have team members share their perspectives on how they intend to accomplish team tasks. For team members with a more Hierarchical Orientation, the leader can state his/her expectation that team members are to describe what they understand the timelines and outcomes to be. It also is helpful to get them to talk about what they will include in their approach.

Notice how the team leader can get to the same outcome with "ask" (Participative) vs. "tell" language (Hierarchical).

This conversation gives team members and the team leader a clearer understanding of task expectations and responsibilities. It requires talking through and asking clarifying questions. Do not leave the asking to the person receiving the instructions, or you may be quite surprised when they do not ask and then do not deliver what is expected.

RECOMMENDED STRATEGIES FOR INFORMATION SHARING

For those with <u>Need for Certainty Orientation</u>:

- Provide details and guidelines whenever strategy or priorities change.

- Communicate regularly, especially in times of crisis. Squelch rumors early and often.

For those with <u>Group Orientation</u>:

- Provide messages that will help them feel connected to the business and financial strategy (for example, the cost of meetings).

For those with <u>Participative Orientation</u>:

- Request and accept suggestions.

- Be a good listener and validate what others have said.

For those with <u>Long-term Orientation</u>:

- Connect disparate ideas or suggestions (for example, say, "This idea is connected to that one…"). NOTE: The ability to think of both/and scenarios rather than either/or is helpful.

Teams are more successful if the team leaders and team members share lots of information. This is particularly difficult for those who like to work quickly and make assumptions that everyone knows what they need to know. Remember, some of the team members may be working in an acquired language and some may need more or less clarification due to their cultural preferences (Need for Certainty or Tolerance for Ambiguity).

When the stakeholders, especially those outside the team and who are at high levels in the company, also communicate with the team, it can make a positive impression and may also make the work more compelling because these stakeholders are "interested in our work." But if the team is working intensively on upcoming important deliverables, it may be wise to reduce communications from the leader and from outside the team for that period.

COMMON GOALS AND PROCESSES

Teams need to know why they are formed. While knowing the end state (target) or outcomes for some is enough, cross-cultural teams often need more. Some cultures are very focused on outcomes; others are more focused on processes. Many cultures need context, which often is missing when defining the mission or vision for the team. The *what* needs to be connected with the *why*.

- Why is the team's work important to the organization?
- Why was I chosen to be part of this team, and what am I expected to deliver?
- Why does the Customer Acceptance Criteria include "a," and why doesn't it include "b"?
- Why do we need to finish in this time frame?
- Why do we have these budget restrictions?

Many Westerners are very comfortable just getting into the work of the team with a brief overview of the project. What often pulls teams apart is the lack of knowledge about what others are doing and the context of the project, as well as clear process steps and explanations...especially the handoffs. Performance targets also need to be clarified and discussed, and if necessary evolved over the performance time period. It should be clear from the outset whether the team itself has control over specific critical decisions or whether these will be made outside the team.

If consistency is a goal (for example, if some of the work is passed on to members in the next time zone all the way around the world to ensure a 24/7 operation), documentation of processes, decisions, and action items can provide the information needed by the team members. If using a framework such as the Project Management Body of Knowledge (PMBOK method), the processes are clearly spelled out for everyone to use.

Whatever method and/or tracking software the team leader chooses for the processes, clarity about what is expected goes a long way to avoiding the need for rework, the potential for miscommunication, and the negative impact that these have on team members. It is very frustrating for those team members who work the second or third shift or remotely to lack information that others have.

Clarifying Goals

Amalie's drug development team had been working to develop several promising compounds over the past nine months. When the senior stakeholder "killed" one of the compounds (stopped funding the research on that compound), the team members working on that chemical combination were stunned.

Impact on the Team

Because Amalie has not clarified the criteria for moving a compound forward (or for killing the compound) the team assumed that the typical time frame of 18 months was going to be acceptable. The members working on that chemical configuration were all of a sudden no longer on the team. This decision by the stakeholder not only stunned them but negatively impacted others on similar teams who no longer felt sure their jobs were safe.

RECOMMENDED STRATEGIES FOR COMMON GOALS AND PROCESSES

For those with **Individual Orientation**:

- Define "commitment to the team." As an example: "We can agree to disagree until a decision is made. Once we all have had our say and a decision is made, we will be expected to support and even champion the decision or approach."

NOTE: You need to make this statement, especially to those with a more Individual Orientation.

For those with **Need for Certainty Orientation**:

- List meeting purposes at the top of the agenda for every meeting. Refer to it when the discussion gets off track, and focus on achieving the purpose at every meeting.

For those with **Achievement Orientation**:

- Make sure all team members can succeed. Make sure they have access to the same technology (and that they are comfortable using it) and that they have access to information about processes, status reports, critical incident reports, etc. Make them aware of how to get the technology help they may need.

Other activities to consider:

- Use culturally appropriate recommendations (given in this book) for team processes.

MANAGING PERFORMANCE

Measuring Team Process

At the beginning of every team meeting, Marieta asks her team members, "So, how are we doing?" Typically she gets a positive answer. When she starts to question this informal approach (answers to which sometimes flew in the face of her own observations), she opts to try a tool that measures team process. The results of the questionnaire are revealing. They showed that there are cracks in the level of trust among team members and that communication is breaking down between some of those at different locations. But team members generally agree that the goals of the team are strategically important to the success of the company.

Impact on the Team

Marieta and a facilitator delivered the results to the team in a three-hour virtual team meeting. Responses from team members linked trust problems to insufficient communications with a portion of the team. Using small group discussions, the team worked out protocols to augment specific team communications. Following the meeting, team members felt they had been given the opportunity to improve process on the team. This relieved many of the tensions that had arisen over communications problems. Using the questionnaire, an instrumented and validated process, the team resolved problems before the productivity of the team was impaired.

It is a team leader's job to make sure people on the team know enough to be able to carry out their responsibilities. How this is handled will depend on the cultural orientation of the team leader and of each team member, as well as the company culture and procedures, but communicating the expectations and the outcomes is a basic need for everyone.

Identifying and Offering Solutions

Jose has just finished a conversation with one of his team members, Carl, who missed an important deadline that caused the delivery time frame to slip. The conversation ended with Jose reminding Carl that he should come to Jose as soon as he identified there might be an issue. He made clear that Carl should think through the possible solutions, present them to Jose, and make a recommendation for how to resolve the issues. Then Jose would help Carl make that decision.

Impact on the Team

Because Carl has a Hierarchical Orientation, he feels very uncomfortable coming to the boss with potential solutions to his challenges. It is his perspective that the team leader should be able to solve problems. Other team members with a more Participative Orientation view Carl as a slacker.

In the case above, where the team leader and the team member have different cultural orientations (Hierarchical or Participative), the team leader should be aware of those differences in order to help Carl and explain those differences. Over time, both Jose and Carl may become more valuable to the organization by learning to apply different cultural approaches on the job. However, it's important to identify if (as in this case) either the Hierarchical or Participative approaches run counter to the culture of the organization. If so, the likelihood is that the approach will not be successful in that organization.

Managing performance should not be a difficult discussion at the end of the year. If done well, it is about a conversation between the team leader and team members throughout the time frame of the project.

How do you know if there is a performance issue? One of the most difficult parts of managing performance is determining whether the employee or team member needs their performance managed or if something else is a better remedy for what is really happening.

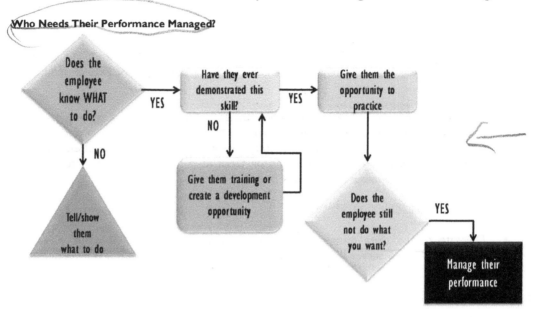

Who Needs Their Performance Managed?

Ask yourself these questions:

Does the employee know what to do? If the answer is no, you need to make sure they know what to do or how to do it. If the answer is yes, they know what to do, then ask yourself this question: Have they ever demonstrated that behavior or skill? If not, give them training or a clearly defined and communicated development opportunity that stresses what they need to learn or do as a result of the opportunity. If the answer is yes, give them opportunities to use and practice that skill, and give them positive feedback when they use or demonstrate it.

If they know what to do, if you know they can do it, and they still do not do what is expected, then you need to manage their performance.

RECOMMENDED STRATEGIES FOR MANAGING PERFORMANCE

For those with **Hierarchical Orientation**:

- Have the leader define acceptable team behavior, leader expectations and outcomes.

For those with **Individual Orientation**:

- Give feedback early and often (including praise where it is due). Catch them doing something right.

NOTE: Individual if giving individual feedback, Group if giving group feedback.

For those with <u>Group Orientation</u>:

- Bestow praise, rewards, or recognition when they are deserved, but do it in a culturally appropriate way (e.g., privately in some cultures; for groups and not individuals in other cultures).

- Review accomplishments, especially when things seem to be dragging; give feedback, especially when expectations are NOT met (do NOT avoid this). Do it in private and in culturally sensitive ways (e.g., approach the issue in a roundabout conversation in Asian cultures but more directly in American or German cultures. Use a mediator or third party to deliver the message, especially in Asia).

For those with <u>Hierarchical Orientation</u>:

- Delegate to the team members the responsibility to provide their input, ideas, and opinions. This also serves as a periodical check-in to see if everyone is still connected to the call.

NOTE: The delegation of this makes it hierarchical as the leader tells team members what is expected.

ye - good pt, way to make of it

MEETING EFFECTIVENESS

When people understand the costs to the company, there is more likely to be an appreciation for why it is important to hold effective meetings. Sometimes conducting an activity to focus on how much of an investment the company makes is eye opening and helps push time spent in meetings to be more effective. There is a simple calculation that defines the direct cost of meetings.

All you need to know is:

- The number of people who attend

- The average compensation costs (per hour) of those who attend

- The regularity of the meeting (weekly or bi-weekly)

- The length of the meeting.

Multiply that all together and you sometimes get an astounding number. Here is an example:

- 15 people attend a weekly meeting

- There are 45 meetings a year

- Their average salary is about $45 an hour

- The meeting is one hour in length.

Multiply 15 people x 45 meetings x one hour each x $45 an hour (the salary costs) and you get over $30,000 per year. Now multiply that by how many different meetings each of these people attends on a weekly basis. If we say five per week, we now are at over $150,000 in direct costs just for meeting time.

What we have not figured into the equation are the following:

- Opportunity Costs – What could these people be doing to expand or extend the business if they were not sitting in this meeting?

- Indirect Costs – Someone outside the team often sets up the room, arranges the calendar (this is very time consuming for large teams), and arranges for technology and perhaps even some food or water.

- Meeting preparation time for all team members.

- Meeting follow-up (documentation and posting).

Some things to consider as you are thinking about how to make meetings more cost effective:

- Make sure those who are invited to attend have a reason to be there. Others who need to know what happened in the meeting may be relieved to find they can get the meeting notes or documentation so they do not have to attend.

- Document a summary of the meeting, decisions made, and action items (see sample below).

- Make sure people who do attend know what is expected of them in advance of the meeting so they can prepare and use their time effectively.

- Send an agenda and put the purpose of the meeting at the top of the agenda to help keep everyone focused on the content.

- Those items that are tangential to the purpose of the meeting need to be captured in the notes or documentation and handled at a different time.

- Start the meeting with restatement of the meeting's purpose.

- Keep the meeting focused on the agenda and the stated purpose.

Ensuring Meeting Effectiveness

Every morning the production meeting is held for all those involved in production and ancillary functions including supply chain, customer service, and finance. The meetings are well attended and everyone thinks the meetings are very important; the client often makes changes on a daily basis, and everyone needs to be kept informed. When the meeting ends, however, attendees often leave with a lack of clarity about who is responsible for the changes discussed.

Impact on the Team

Since the meeting happens every day, the meeting leader assumes that there is no need for either an agenda or written documentation of action items. This causes duplication of efforts (more than one person thinks they are responsible) or things that are dropped (everyone thinks others are responsible to get that done). The team members distrust each other and some perceive that others "get away" without being held accountable, which causes dissatisfaction among team members.

The team leader is missing an opportunity to provide clarity and structure, to reduce rework and to ensure the work changes are handled quickly so the customer is satisfied. Even if they use a standing agenda (for example, every day we will summarize what we were able to accomplish and discuss the challenges that we are presented with today), the documentation of action items is critical to effective meetings.

Reviewing a list of outstanding items from previous meetings (Need for Certainty):

- Ensures the tasks are accomplished

- Improves scheduling of downstream activities

- Holds people accountable for the commitments they made to finalize the task

- Identifies barriers

- Provides an opportunity to discuss problem solutions (short-term)

- Identifies recurring problems that can be fixed with process changes.

The documentation of decisions made and action items frames the agenda for the next meeting, keeps those who could not attend informed, and helps keep the meetings on track (Need for Certainty).

Sample Documentation Format

Team Name:_____

Project	
Document Date	
Author	
Topic	
Audience	
Action Request	

Summary of Meeting Topics:

Outcomes – Decisions Made:

Outcomes – Action Item(s), who is responsible, and timelines:

RECOMMENDED STRATEGIES FOR MEETING EFFECTIVENESS

For those with Group Orientation:

- Acknowledge to the team that being virtual might have a negative impact on meeting effectiveness unless specific processes are adopted.

For those with <u>Need for Certainty Orientation</u>:

- Acknowledge that more up-front planning and preparation for participants (pre-reading, presentation assignments, etc.) is required for remote meetings.

- Use a standardized format for documenting decisions, open items, and action items.

For more information, go to Chapter 5: Leading Effective Meetings.

SPECIFIC ASPECTS OF THE CULTURAL ORIENTATIONS NAMED IN THIS CHAPTER

Individualism Orientation	A preference for working alone or to advance oneself. Task prevails over relationship.
Group Orientation	Team purposes are raised above individual needs. Relationship prevails over task.
Hierarchical Orientation	Work tasks are clearly presented; employees expect to be told what to do; top top-down organization.
Participative Orientation	Subordinates expect to be consulted; good ideas and suggestions can come from any organizational level; matrix or flat structures.
Need for Certainty Orientation	There is a more formal and widely understood way of getting things done; there is comfort in structured situations; managers are expected to have the answers.
Tolerance for Ambiguity	Comfort with ambiguous situations; trying new approaches is encouraged; rewards may be given for "thinking outside the box."
Achievement Orientation	Assertiveness, competitiveness, and ambition are virtues.

These are very useful categories

Chapter 10
Strengthening Team Communication, Part 1

Communication involves both sending and receiving information. The purpose of communicating is to build understanding. To promote understanding, sending information is not only about content. It is also about context as well as the medium used to send the message. Even if we are clear about the content and provide context to improve understanding to someone who prefers relationship to task, using a medium such as email may seem impersonal and perhaps even rude. Offer a telephone or in-person conversation with anyone who wants to take the opportunity to seek clarification.

Communication is one of the most critical responsibilities of team leaders. When in cross-cultural and or cross-functional teams, the most important tasks include:

1. **Keep stakeholders informed.** This includes members of the team as well as project boards, customers, and other organizational stakeholders. Communicate early and often, making sure even functional leaders who have staff represented on the teams know what is happening and the status of team activities.

2. **Explain why.** We communicate with others and often do not explain why we are sending the message, why this content is important, and why we are sending it now. Including this information is what is known as "building verbal bridges" between concepts so that there are no gaps in understanding.

3. **Seek feedback to make sure you are understood.** Once something is said, written, or sent, it is helpful to check to make sure the receiver has understood what the sender meant to convey. Having a conversation helps reduce misunderstandings, and it makes the communication two-way, not just one-way.

4. **Make the medium appropriate to the message.** Email is the least personal approach, and it does not include any voice inflection or body language that could help the receiver understand the message.

5. **Seek to express, not to impress.** The use of functional acronyms impedes communication. Use of unusual or rarely used words may impress those who speak the same language you do, but this may impede the understanding of those who acquired this language.

6. **Recognize the difference between an inductive and a deductive approach.** Some cultures are more direct or linear in their communication, but others are less direct. Information presented either inductively or deductively needs to be acceptable and welcomed as well as understood.

7. **Explain why certain approaches are necessary on cross-cultural teams.** Help your team members become more culturally proficient by explaining activities within a cultural context.

Communication includes sending messages (speaking, emails, telephone conversations, meeting interactions), receiving messages (reading, listening), and questioning techniques. When done well, communication can help build trust, ensure team focus (through message clarity), and develop camaraderie within the team. Inadequate, infrequent, or unclear communication erodes trust, demotivates team members, and impedes progress towards achievement of project deliverables.

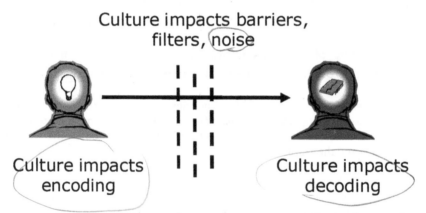

Culture impacts barriers, filters, noise

Culture impacts encoding

Culture impacts decoding

Communication is about sending and receiving messages. Both the sender and the receiver filter the message and culture impacts how they encode or decode it.

In addition, anything that interferes with the sending or receiving is called "noise" or is referred to as static.

Static can be caused by many things: Lack of language facility on either the sender's or the receiver's part, interpretive failures, a failure to listen on the part of the receiver, a mismatch between abilities either to express or to understand complex messages, lack of trust between sender and receiver, or style differences in how messages are expressed and heard, among other causes. Interpretative failures are often the result of cultural differences, but they may also be caused by personality differences or problems with the message or the choice of the medium of communication.

Effective communication:

- Involves understanding what method of communication is best for a given situation
- Requires clear expression of information, intent, and goals
- Involves following up to make sure that the message was understood as it was intended.

Team leaders need to manage the internal communication challenges but also should not neglect the communication with those outside the team.

COMMUNICATIONS EXTERNAL TO THE TEAM

Keeping external stakeholders informed is just as important as communications within the team. In addition to managing the team, team leaders need to manage up (to their superiors) and out (to other stakeholders).

Communicating with Stakeholders

Macon's team deliverables schedule has slipped. He estimates that he needs an additional three weeks from the two programmers on his team in order to ensure that the testing process is completed before customer delivery. He goes to the head of Research and Development to ask for an extension for the programmers and finds out that this extension is practically impossible. One of the programmers has been assigned to another team in a different location and will have to relocate for three months, and the other is scheduled for a training delivery in India during that time.

Impact on the Team

The team, which has worked hard to get to this point, is now left without key members (the programmers). This is due in part to the team leader's failure to keep to the agreed timeline and the team leader's and functional leaders' failure to inform each other of schedules and assignments. This hurts the team leader's reputation both inside and outside the team. It may also damage the reputation of the company if testing is not completed before customer delivery. Team members become frustrated that the impact of this situation may overshadow all the hard work it took to get the project close to completion.

Functional managers of the team members are often not included in team communications. Stakeholders may find value in information on status updates, slipped deadlines, and the need for additional resources. Of course, functional managers should also help team leaders with resources to complete the team's mission and keep team leaders informed of resource changes that will impact the team.

WHO NEEDS TO KNOW?

Who needs to be informed? How much information do they need? How often do they need to hear from the team or team leader? If there is a project management board or sponsorship board, these stakeholders will have a say in the resources and funding of the project. Keep them informed of both successes and evolving resource needs. Line managers and other subject matter experts (SMEs) who may be brought into the team during specific stages should also be included in external communications. (Take, for example, a marketing resource who might only be part of the team during the Customer Acceptance Criteria development stage and then towards the end of the project when the product or service is mature enough to begin the development of a marketing strategy and collateral materials.)

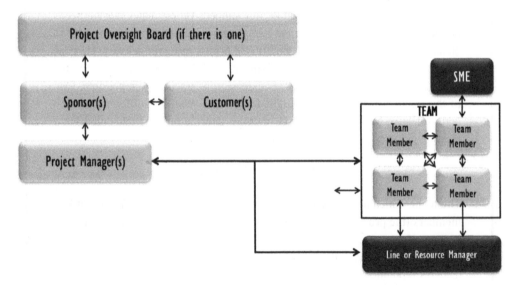

Establishment of a communication plan makes sure everyone who needs to be informed (especially those paying for the work of the team) is kept informed. Your plan should include a list of those with a need to know, and what and when and how they should receive the information. Interviews with stakeholders can provide the information needed to conduct a stakeholder analysis and create a communication plan. (A stakeholder is any person or organization that is actively involved in the project or whose interests may be positively or negatively affected by execution or completion of the project. Stakeholders often exert influence over the project and its deliverables.)

Not every stakeholder needs to know everything. In fact, some do not care to be as involved as others. It is important to:

- Determine who needs to be kept informed about what transpires and who needs how much detail vs. an overview.

- Determine how often to communicate and using what medium.

- Identify the objectives of each communication, the appropriate medium, and the appropriate frequency of the communication for each stakeholder.

- Validate the communication plan with the stakeholders and assign accountability within the team to ensure the communication plan is followed.

- Document what has been communicated to whom.

See below for how to compare the level of power to the level of interest each stakeholders has. This will help you determine the contents of the communication plan.

WHO ARE THE PROJECT STAKEHOLDERS?

There are various types of possible stakeholders:

1. Any internal or external customer (the person, department or group who will be the end user of the project outcomes);

2. The internal sponsor (typically the person or department who is either the champion for the project or responsible to fund the project);

3. Any process owner (a department involved in any process that is affected by the project, or resource provider, or person representing a department or function);

4. Any external supplier; and/or

5. Any external regulatory or compliance body.

In order to identify (and make a list of) project stakeholders, ask yourself the following questions:

- Who owns or will own the new process, service, or product?

- Whose budget will fund this project?

- Who will be affected by:
  o the project
  o the resources needed to complete the project
  o the project's outcomes or deliverables?

You can create a table like the one below to help the team keep track of interactions with the stakeholders.

Stakeholder type	Stakeholder name	How affected by the project	Requirements or concerns	Team liaison to that stakeholder	Frequency and type of communication preferred	Date(s) contacted

WHY IS IT IMPORTANT?

Some people assume that if they hear nothing that all is going well. Others assume if they hear nothing that things are not moving forward at all. Err on the side of communicating more rather than less.

The lack of effective external communication may cause rework due to:

- A change in strategic priorities

- Lack of clarity around outcome requirements

- Loss of funding

- Lack of confidence in the team leader and/or the team

- Budget overruns

- Missed milestones.

Remember to communicate with external audiences about milestones met and other successes. This positive communication also helps the team members:

- Recognize that the team leader is advocating for them

- Know what they can talk about external to the team with non-stakeholders

- Develop a sense of satisfaction by knowing the schedule for how well the team is moving forward towards completion. (This is especially valuable for those whose orientation is Need for Certainty.)

HOW DO YOU WORK WITH STAKEHOLDERS TO CREATE A PLAN?

Once you have identified stakeholders, work with each to gather information that can be used to create a stakeholder map. It is this information that will become the basis of your communication plan. Stakeholder maps (see sample below) are used to:

- Assess how interested the stakeholders are in the project

- Identify and rate stakeholders' attitudes (from "strongly in favor/high interest" to "strongly opposed/low interest")

- Analyze how much power and influence each stakeholder has over the project or decisions about the project (from "can veto/high power" to "not much influence/low power")

- Form the type and frequency of stakeholder communication.

Put names in the appropriate boxes and post the results of the interviews and analysis on a grid like this one. As you can see, once you put the names in the box that describes their level of influence and interest, there is a recommendation for communication to them. What is not included, because this will differ by stakeholder and may be influenced by their cultural preferences, is the method they prefer you to use to keep them informed. Some will want in-person meetings, some may prefer email, and others may be willing to go to the team repository for materials. Make sure when you are interviewing the stakeholders, you ask them how they wish to be updated (which method) and how often.

HIGH		
	High Level of Power/Influence Low Level of Interest	High Level of Power/Influence High Level of Interest
LEVEL OF POWER/INFLUENCE	Low Level of Power/Influence Low Level of Interest	Low Level of Power/Influence High Level of Interest
LOW	**LEVEL OF INTEREST**	HIGH

Here is some advice on how to work with and communicate to the people whose names fall into one of these boxes:

- Those in the upper left quadrant (high level of influence, low level of interest) are people to convince. They need to be kept satisfied, so do what you must do to meet their communication and information needs.

- Those in the lower left quadrant (low level of influence, low level of interest) are probably minor skeptics. Monitor their needs, but you can make less of an effort with these people.

- Those in the lower right quadrant (low level of influence, high level of interest) can be change facilitators for you due to their level of interest. Keep them informed and show consideration to their communication needs.

- Those in the upper right quadrant (high level of influence, high level of interest) are to be considered key players. They can be change agents. Manage the communication with them very closely.

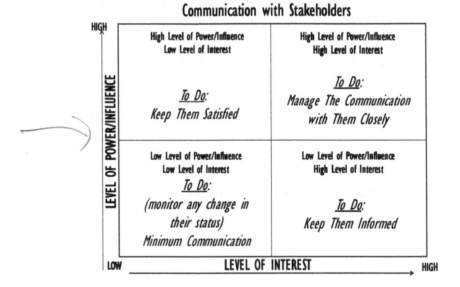

Communication with Stakeholders

	HIGH	
	High Level of Power/Influence Low Level of Interest	High Level of Power/Influence High Level of Interest
	To Do: *Keep Them Satisfied*	*To Do:* *Manage The Communication* *with Them Closely*
LEVEL OF POWER/INFLUENCE	Low Level of Power/Influence Low Level of Interest *To Do:* *(monitor any change in* *their status)* *Minimum Communication*	Low Level of Power/Influence High Level of Interest *To Do:* *Keep Them Informed*
LOW	LEVEL OF INTEREST	HIGH

Team leaders are responsible for external communication in order to:

- Keep stakeholders informed (this of course includes team members)

- Champion the team's work and the individual contributions of team members

- Remove barriers and secure resources (such as time, budget, people, tools)

- Gain recognition for team and team members (lessons learned, innovations)

- Explain and celebrate milestone achievements.

COMMUNICATIONS INTERNAL TO THE TEAM

Team leaders with Participative and Tolerance for Ambiguity Orientations often expect team members to raise issues, ask questions, and come up with solutions that are different from the way things are typically done. This behavior can be difficult for team members who have a more Hierarchical Orientation. Their perception may be that it is the team leader's job to identify issues and solutions.

Team leaders with Hierarchical and Need for Certainty Orientation often are surprised (and may feel it is inappropriate behavior) when team members raise issues, ask questions, and come up with solutions that are different from the way things are typically done. On the other hand, if a team leader reacts negatively to a comment, situation, or difficulty with what might be perceived as a lack of openness, team members with a more Participative Orientation and Tolerance for Ambiguity Orientations may consider this a failure of leadership.

Since problem solving is one of the activities that teams typically face, some thought should be given to different styles of problem solving. Here are some strategies for Participative leaders working with team members with a stronger Hierarchical Orientation:

1. Delegate (a more hierarchical behavior) the responsibility of asking questions.

2. Use "tell" rather than "ask" approaches. For example, "Please do x" or "do x" is a "tell" approach while "Would you please do x?" or "Can you please do x?" is an "ask" approach.

3. When team members demonstrate the behaviors desired, recognize and reinforce it. This will help other team members:
   a. Understand better what is accepted and expected
   b. Learn how to work outside their preference
   c. Take the opportunity to practice working counter to their preferred orientation. (See Part III for instructor guides for various team activities.)

ESTABLISHING A TEAM OPERATING AGREEMENT/TEAM CHARTER

The first official team meeting can be used as a team chartering opportunity or to set a team operating agreement. These kinds of documents can help make sure all team members are focused on goals, objectives, and common processes from the start. It can provide a big picture overview, which is especially valuable to those team members who either have a need for certainty or who need a high level of context. Whether you call it a charter or an operating agreement, the purpose of the document is to establish the parameters of the project. It should be drawn up and presented when the team is first formed.

How the team comes to agreement will depend on the cultural orientations of the team members and the leader. A more hierarchical leader will *tell* whereas a more participative leader will *ask* and involve team members in establishing or refining the agreement.

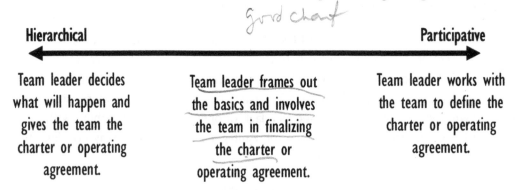

Good chart

Hierarchical		Participative
Team leader decides what will happen and gives the team the charter or operating agreement.	Team leader frames out the basics and involves the team in finalizing the charter or operating agreement.	Team leader works with the team to define the charter or operating agreement.

How a leader achieves agreement should depend in part on the cultural orientations of the team members. One of the ways to ensure even those with a Group Orientation get involved is to put the team members into small groups. Have the groups come up with questions to ensure clarity and to identify barriers. The leader also can ask the small groups to identify topics that the leader needs to know about or think about in order to make the plan successful.

Operating agreements can be complex and include all sorts of information such as the roles of each members, the team leader, and all stakeholders, as well as all protocols: communication, meeting times/dates/typical content, and acceptable behaviors of team members towards each other (such as how fast they are expected to respond even if they do not yet have an answer).

Even if the operating agreement is simple, it should at least include the purpose of the team, what the goals or outcomes are, when and/or how often they will meet, and how documents and communications are going to be handled.

Clarity around purpose, goals, outcomes, and milestones goes a long way to establishing the team members' understanding of priorities, dates, and deliverables. See below for a simple agreement that helps create a clear target for teams.

Sample: Simple Team Operating Agreement

TOPIC	DESCRIPTION	AGREEMENT
Purpose and overall goals (High level description of outcome desired)	The purpose of the _____ team is to _____ so that_____.	During team chartering meeting; post on the repository
Objectives (measureable results)	SMART Objectives	During team chartering meeting; post on the repository
Meetings	For example, "Weekly; each Tuesday for 45 minutes." We will rotate times so that those members who work in remote locations are not always in meetings before or after work hours.	Put on a joint calendar
Agendas, Documents, Reports, etc.	Post and/or read prior to each meeting.	Post on the team's electronic repository
Establish communication protocols information	Email subject line, response time, who gets cc'ed, when response is needed by, what if the time frame cannot be met, etc.	During team chartering meeting; post on the repository

The precise format of team charters will vary. The value of a charter comes from thinking through and stating the various elements. These elements might include the following:

1. The purpose of the team activities.

2. The expected duration of the project and of particular team members' time commitment.

3. The scope of the deliverables (what is in scope and what is out of scope).

4. The members of the team and other stakeholders.

5. The desired end result and the "customer" who needs these deliverables.

6. The internal and external resources that will be available to team members (e.g., staff support, communication technologies, etc.).

7. The communication plan and links to technology as well as technical experts.

8. The calendar with specific deliverables and milestones.

Development of this draft document prior to the first team meeting gives the project leader a lot of preparatory work. It is likely that the finalization of all these topics will happen with the support of the team members either during or following the charter (first) meeting.

This becomes the "roadmap" for the team to follow to make sure all (including stakeholders) are clear about where the journey will lead.

The chartering meeting should be introduced by one or more of the sponsors to provide legitimacy. This also helps those with a strong Hierarchical Orientation. This is especially important if there are team members who have a higher title or more respected professions than the person chosen to lead the team.

Demonstrating Leadership Effectiveness

Jana is a very well-respected nurse who is tasked with leading a drug regulatory approval preparation team. On her team of 18 people are three doctors. No senior sponsor attended the team charter meeting. The doctors find it difficult to report to a nurse and complain to her supervisor that she is not an effective team leader.

Impact on the Team

Jana has to call in consultants to assess the human process interactions on the team to demonstrate to her sponsor that the issue is caused by her profession being considered a "lower level" one by the doctors and not caused by ineffective team leadership. Even though the assessment proved she was effective as a leader, the team lost time and money dealing with what should have been a non-issue.

At least some of the activities in the initial meeting should include the results of team member conversations and small group discussions about establishing measurable objectives, protocols, time zones, preferences for how to receive contact, work and vacation schedules, and preferred method of communication (email voicemail, mobile, IM, etc.). These work best for those with Group and Quality of Life Orientations. Including activities in meetings that allow team members to get to know each other better helps build relationships (Group Orientation) and trust. It also is appropriate for those with Quality of Life orientations because it helps to develop a more collegial working environment. Members with a higher Individualism and or Achievement Orientation can be those who speak up and report out of the smaller groups.

Too often team members and team leaders are eager to start work right away and do not spend sufficient time clearly setting objectives and providing context. This lack of planning is likely to result in a less productive team throughout the term of the project.

Effective teams are better at avoiding rework. Rework often is caused by missed communications: misunderstandings, lack of clarity about what needs to be done, lack of clarity about deliverable dates, lack of clarity about customers' acceptance criteria, withholding information, providing data not synthesized into useful information, slow turnaround time on responses, and so forth. The goal is to avoid rework, which means spending the time to plan is critical to the success of a project.

The Goal is to Avoid Rework

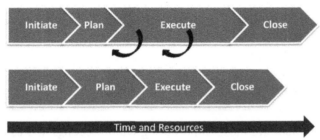

In addition to establishing relationships and distributing contact information, another of the outcomes of this meeting is a general agreement and understanding about how the team members will operate. Below is a set of team activities. Many are aligned with one or more cultural orientation. Most team leaders and team members do not already know the cultural preferences of the others, so think of these lists as a toolbox of approaches to try in order to be culturally sensitive. If one approach does not work well, try another.

The other option is to conduct an assessment of the team members' cultural profiles in order to improve team effectiveness through providing team members with a high level of cultural competency. Please see Chapter 21 for more information about how to assess team members' cultural preferences.

RECOMMENDED STRATEGIES FOR ESTABLISHING EFFECTIVE TEAM MEETINGS

For those with Need for Certainty Orientation:

- Establish how often meetings should take place and at what time(s). Do not meet for meeting's sake. Make sure for each session that there is a planned meeting outcome that is communicated to stakeholders in advance.

- Create protocols such as:
    - Decide on appropriate request response times
    - Establish a special reserved time at the beginning and end of the meeting for technology setup, testing, and break down
    - In written communications, use sub-headings to clarify new topics
    - Provide written text and visuals to illustrate your message
    - Determine the time frame for notes to be distributed.

For those with Hierarchical Orientation:

- Explain your expectations for who should speak at meetings. Will you use a "roll call" system (calling on each person by geography) when in person, virtual, or both?

For those with Group Orientation:

- Provide short bios with work and personal data (that participants supply), pictures, and contact information to help establish relationships.

ESTABLISHING COMMUNICATION AND OTHER TEAM PROTOCOLS

Team members communicate most often during team meetings and as a follow-up to the action items discussed in teams. They need to know that they can contact each other directly any time. For example, those with a Hierarchical Orientation may feel it is more appropriate to go through channels or ask permission from the team leader before they contact a team member who is at a higher level in the organization. One of the protocols could include a waiver on going through channels. yes

It is likely that most meetings will be virtual, which adds the complexity of technology to already challenging circumstances for team leaders and team members.

While a lot of meeting strategies are "common sense," many of them also have a cultural or language rationale. For example:

- Prior to each meeting, determine who needs to attend based on the agenda of topics to be covered. Not everyone may need to attend every meeting, although everyone should be informed of the meeting (Need for Certainty) to avoid the notion that non-invitees have been kept out of the information stream.

- Inform in advance those who will be asked to present to the group and provide each with a time frame for their portion of the agenda. (This helps those who will be presenting and gives a structure to the meeting content for those with a higher Need for Certainty.) It also gives all team members a sense of the purpose and framework for the meeting.

- Sending out an agenda in advance (at least eight "work hours" for attendees around the world) and following up with action items after the meeting are good practices. Both also are very helpful to those who speak acquired languages.
  - o Having the agenda in advance gives them time to mentally prepare for the topics to be covered in the meeting and to prepare their questions.
  - o Providing written meeting summaries helps diverse members check their understanding of meeting outcomes. These should include:
    - Summary notes on what was discussed
    - What decisions were made and which issues closed
    - Outstanding issues
    - Upcoming action items (who is responsible and by when)
    - The next meeting date
    - It may also be useful to send out the timeline developed for the team charter indicating which items have been delivered on time, which are late, and any changes in the timing of deliverables.

- Explain how you are going to invite comments and suggestions. For example, if you are using roll call they will not be surprised. NOTE: This technique is especially useful on teleconferences. The team leader can explain by saying, "I am going to call on each of you to give you an opportunity to express your opinion and share your ideas." The team leader then calls on each of them by name. This allows the leader to make sure everyone gets a chance to speak (especially those from cultures of silence who do not interrupt others) and has the added benefit of making sure no one sits quietly by or is multi-tasking (or has gotten dropped off) during a conference call.

Communicating Upcoming Events

Maya, who has a stronger orientation towards Need for Certainty, finds project meetings without agendas to be extremely frustrating and disorganized. She does not respect the team leader, whom Maya sees as disorganized because she runs meetings too loosely. Maya feels that little is accomplished in the meetings. All that happens is idea generation, and while ideas are raised for discussion, decisions are not made.

Impact on the Team

Such team leaders may be perceived as lacking leadership. Team members may be surprised and embarrassed by being called on for their opinion when they are not prepared and may no longer fully trust the team leader.

What happens in the meetings will depend on the type and purpose of the meeting. Here are some examples of the types of meetings and the typical outcomes expected:

TYPE	OUTCOME
Team Chartering meeting	Agreement on the team charter
Planning meeting	Plan
Decision making	Decision/Actions
Problem solving	Solution or approaches
Monitoring of status	Report on status
Working meeting	Finalizing deliverables
Kick-off meeting	Launch (a product, a team, a project)
Lessons learned	Codifying approaches for other teams to use

Effective strategies to keep focus on the meeting agenda include:

- Send a meeting agenda in advance.

- On the top of the agenda, include the names of the invitees and the time the meeting is for them in their time zones.

- List the meeting purpose at the top of the agenda. You can also post this in the room if the meeting is not virtual or on the materials handed out or sent for review.

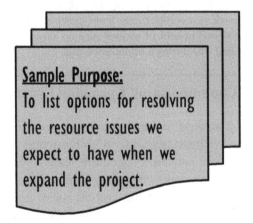

Sample Purpose:
To list options for resolving the resource issues we expect to have when we expand the project.

Keeping the focus on the purpose of the meeting will allow the team leader to postpone any topics that arise if those topics do not drive the meeting participants to achieve the stated purpose. These items can be put on the "outstanding items" (or "parking lot") list for inclusion on the agendas of future meetings.

Effective use of team meeting time may include:

1. Monitoring the project.
   - Are there difficulties meeting timelines?
   - Have any resources been added or lost?
   - Have priorities changed?
   - Are there new barriers/issues/problems/risks?
   - What is the status of previously identified issues/problems/risks?

2. Facilitating communication between team members and team leader.

3. Managing and communicating the changes to the project plan, especially if things have changed in the environment (internal or external to the team).

Team leaders can also use each team meeting as an opportunity to build relationships between team members. Set the stage by including in your agenda a "milestones" segment. Everyone is asked to offer milestone(s) that have occurred since the previous meeting. These can be personal or professional. As a leader you need to model how to share both personal and professional milestones. This will "give permission" for the milestones segments to include both work and/or personal information.

Use this opportunity to ask about happenings in various locations, especially where it shows concern for team members (such as a sports event or current event like a typhoon that will affect members in a specific location). Vary your comments and questions so you do not have to spend time with each team member in each meeting. Ask similar questions and show similar concerns and knowledge about what is going on in the remote locations when you communicate with team members between meetings. Make sure you update the whole team where appropriate.

Opening the meeting consists of a set of topics that could include:

- Determining how you are going to keep a "parking lot" for ideas and topics for later discussion. (NOTE: The term "parking lot" may not translate into anything meaningful for most people who speak an acquired language. Explain that this means the team will create and sometimes post a list of things that come up in meetings that will be held for a later discussion or meeting.)

- Greetings by name as people enter the room or sign on to the technology being used.

- Introductions/Roll call.

- Review of the Agenda/Logistics.

- Milestones – Ask members to share their personal and professional milestones since the last conversation.

- Other content as described on the agenda – especially if there are changes to the agenda.

ASSESSING THE RISKS AND PROJECT CONSTRAINTS

Team members often focus on the tasks but not on the overall picture. Early in the life of the team, it is important for team members to gain an appreciation of all the project tasks and risks.

Clearly there may be personal risks of failure that affect the team members' and team leader's reputation and pay scale. In addition, there are risks to the reputation of the business or function and to the financial future of the company.

Such a risk is any potential event that can trigger a negative effect on team members, the team, and its work, or on the business and its stakeholders. Conducting a risk assessment helps teams identify and analyze any potential problem so that risk-mitigating approaches can be included in the project plan. These assessments can help:

- Determine what risks exist

- Identify how to counter or prevent risks

- Add to the project plan tasks that mitigate risks

- Communicate to the organization the risks and countermeasures needed.

In addition to team members, there are others who probably should be included in the discussion about risks. These could include:

- Stakeholders

- IT technical experts (such as security, applications, architecture)

- Sponsors and customers

- Skeptics (for example, any person who did not want the project approved to begin with)

- Subject Matter Experts (SMEs).

You may wish to begin with a review of the triple constraint (see diagram). Talk about how every project has competing demands—cost, timing and scope of the outcomes. One can typically get more of one of these at the expense of the other. For example, to achieve the project deliverables faster you might need more resources which increases the cost. For cheaper costs, the project might have to change to a reduced scope.

A triple constraint is depicted as a triangle representing the parameters being managed by the project team: schedule, cost and scope. Project quality is affected by balancing these three factors. Discuss any risks that could harm the final deliverables.

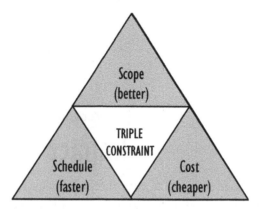

Make sure that each component of the triple constraint is considered. Consider things such as:

- Inability to meet Customer Acceptance Criteria (CAC)
- Deadlines
- Budget constraints.

Strive for quantity of risks over quality, and remember, correct identification of risk allows the team to use the countermeasures to those risks that could reduce project time!

It is important to know your sponsor's perspectives on which of these is most important and why...and the stakeholders' tolerance for failure for each of these project requirements.

You also could list the sponsor's priorities (Priority 1, P2, P3), which is what the Sponsor would prefer if s/he could have the following: more features (better), completed ahead of schedule (faster), or completed for less money (cheaper). In some cases, it is necessary to ask which one is least important to achieve.

PROBABILITY/IMPACT ANALYSIS

To finalize the assessment, conducting a Probability/Impact Matrix will help identify the priorities of your countermeasures. See the example on the following page.

Probability

	Low	Medium	High
High			
Medium			
Low			

Impact

Hold a discussion about how they would rate the probability of each risk (high, medium, or low probability). Also rate the impact to the project if that risk were to occur. You can use a post-It note such as in this graphic. In this example the probability is rated low (L).

It is the judgment call of the group to decide the probability and impact and where the post-its will go on the table. For example, a risk with High Probability and Medium Impact would be posted in the top center as in this graphic.

Probability

	Low	Medium	High
High		P = H I = M Risk Description	
Medium			
Low			

Impact

Evaluate the countermeasures based on their merit and how realistic they are. Consider:

- Ease
- Cost
- Impact.

Select the countermeasures the group agrees should actually be used. Types of countermeasures might include doing **something to mitigate the risk** (for example, arranging for back-up resources). It might be to **avoid the risk** (for example, choosing a different approach). The decision might be to **get insurance** (to mitigate part of the effect). Or of course, you could **accept the risk** (for example, there may be nothing you can or that you choose to do). Then designate a resource to be accountable to ensure each risk is monitored and each countermeasure is enacted. (For example, if you have three countermeasures, you may have three different names of resources.)

Often it helps to link the roles or tasks of team members so they can visualize the handoffs and dependent variables. You can do this by creating a visual/flow chart to help those working in an acquired language. Make sure you warn the stakeholder of the risk, especially if the stakeholders have a low risk threshold (a strong Need for Certainty Orientation).

INTERNAL TEAM COMMUNICATION

Sometimes team members do not speak up during virtual meetings. There may be several reasons for this. For example:

- People in remote locations may be working very late in their day or at night and find it more difficult to express themselves in an acquired language when they are tired. Rotating the meeting times every time can reduce this problem.

- Those team members with Hierarchical Orientations may defer to their superiors rather than risk disagreeing with them. In this case, it is important to hold back the team leader's opinion and learn to ask carefully crafted questions.

- Technical problems may have caused dropped communications.

- Sometimes they need a little encouragement (Participative Orientation).

- They may need to be told that expressing themselves is a behavior expected by the team leader (Hierarchical Orientation).

- Sometimes small group work is preferred for expressing opinions (Group Orientation).

ASKING EFFECTIVE QUESTIONS *yes, good*

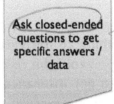

Ask open-ended questions to probe for further information

Ask closed-ended questions to get specific answers / data

When asked a content question ask, "What do you think?" or "What does the group think?"

Ask questions for clarification or to provoke more critical thinking

Open-ended questions easily encourage those with Individual and Participative Orientations to respond. After some suggestions, ideas, or perspectives have been offered, probe those being quiet by asking direct open-ended questions. Allow them time to think before they respond. "How would that work?" or "What ideas can you share that we should consider?" are examples. Some team members may make great contributions to a team's work but not express themselves well verbally.

For those from Hierarchical cultures, they may need to be called upon to answer a question. They may respond if they are told that it is the team leader's expectation that everyone comment or provide an answer. Team members who have been socialized with a Group Orientation may have difficulties expressing their individual opinion.

Those with a Need for Certainty can respond more effectively if they are given notice in advance that they are going to be called upon and what kind of response is acceptable. For example, a team leader might say, "I am going to call on each of you by name. I want to hear everyone's comments on this idea. Feel free to elaborate on other ideas, ask questions, or concur with the approach we are discussing." This allows others who are initially less comfortable giving their opinion the chance to add their voices.

Closed-ended questions are useful to get specific data. "When was that decided?" or "Do you think that would solve the problem?" are examples.

Feel free to encourage people to add on to what others said, be creative with existing ideas, or modify ideas slightly. You might say, "This idea seems interesting. What can you add to this idea to make the solution even more effective or efficient?" Another approach might be to say, "Ok, we have two ideas here to consider. How could we do both?" Western cultures tend to encourage "either/or" thinking, while Asian cultures are more adept at synthetic ("both/and") thinking.

Of course not all communication is face-to-face. This chapter provides some strategies for using technology. It also focuses on how to achieve clarity with scope, and end barriers to effective communication and communication protocols.

VIDEO AND TELE-CONFERENCING

Since most virtual team meetings are held using video or teleconferencing, here are some strategy recommendations for each.

RECOMMENDED STRATEGIES FOR VIDEO AND TELE-CONFERENCING

For those with Need for Certainty Orientation:

- Join the conference in advance of the meeting start time to make sure the equipment is working properly.

- Ask everyone to start the call three minutes early to check their connectivity.

- Use technology support personnel until you are very comfortable with the equipment.

- Have protocols for how to restart the call (if necessary) or reconnect someone dropped from the call.

- Remind everyone to mute their microphone because video conference equipment picks up voice as well as any ambient noise (from paper rattling or coughing, to air conditioning/heating noises or even traffic noises) and will cause the camera to focus on the location that has either voice or any noise.

- Remind the attendees that they should assume that they are always on camera in case the visuals jump to their location due to ambient noise.

- Have speakers look at the camera so others can see them. This assists other language speakers in understanding speech.

- If it's audio only, and/or the people are new or just have met, they should be asked to state their names when they speak so others can get to know/recognize them.

For those with Group Orientation:

- Start the meeting with updates and milestones. These can be work-related, but encourage other updates (births, celebrations, holidays, etc.) to help build relationships between remote team members.

- Ask everyone to speak distinctly and for some, more slowly so that everyone can understand what is being said.

- If the team cannot ever get together face-to-face, use a photo gallery with short bios including work information and whatever personal data they are culturally comfortable sharing. This helps them get to know more about each other and builds group trust.

For those with Quality of Life Orientation:

- Periodically ask questions and call on each location. This keeps everyone participating, lets them know you are thinking about their needs, and helps you know that all locations are online.

- Have backup communications approaches when someone's connection gets dropped (e.g., the one who was dropped can text a message to someone other than the leader of the meeting).

USING EMAIL

Even though teams admit that email is the worst communication medium to use for building trust and relationships, most teams rely heavily on email communication.

Copying People on Email Messages

The Spanish members of a pharmaceutical research and development team copied their functional managers on all team correspondence.

Impact on the Team

Their American colleagues viewed this behavior with skepticism. It made them wonder if their Spanish colleagues did not trust them. The Spanish members felt it was important to keep the boss informed (Hierarchical Orientation) and felt that their American colleagues were trying to hide something when they did not cc: their supervisors.

In this case it was not the message that created the problem but who was included on the distribution list. The Spanish colleagues were copying their functional managers out of respect for their position (Hierarchical Orientation). The Americans (Participative Orientation) thought that including the functional managers was totally unnecessary since their managers trusted them to represent the function on that team.

Sometimes it is important to have a record of conversations and decisions. Email is very useful for sharing documentation of decisions and action items (fact sharing). Email distribution is a more effective first step if the second step includes posting documentation in a repository that team members can access and review.

While in certain instances, such as sharing facts, written messages can be effective for a team, using a written message could cause a misinterpretation. Important issues should be discussed face-to-face or over the telephone. Quick yet important messages can be sent in emails or chats, but there should be some sort of verbal follow-up to ensure the correct and full meaning was received.

Team members receive so many emails daily that some agreement about how to use the subject line of emails can help the receivers determine the priority of the message.

RECOMMENDED STRATEGIES FOR USING EMAIL

For those with **Need for Certainty Orientation**:

- Create a protocol for use of the SUBJECT line to help priority setting. You might use the following:
    - ACTION REQUIRED: means "I need you to pay attention to this as a high priority," and your protocol would be to also insert the time frame and deliverable in the subject line
    - ACTION REQUESTED: means "I need this from you" or "you need to take some action on this"
    - FOR YOUR INFORMATION: means "I thought this might interest you" or "you need to know this but not necessarily take any action."

For those with **Hierarchical Orientation**:

- Identify who should be included on the distribution list for which kinds of emails.

- A more hierarchical approach is to list by level in the organization with higher level people first.

- Do not be too casual. Some cultures prefer a bit more formality. Agree upon a salutation and closing that is acceptable protocol for the team and encourage its use.

For those with Participative Orientation:

- Identify who should be included on the distribution list for which kinds of emails.

- A more participative approach would be to list people alphabetically by last name or to group people's names by function.

Other Strategies:

- Keep messages, sentences, and structure simple.

- Use sub-headings to highlight a change of topic—this is especially useful for non-native speakers as it helps them understand when the topic has changed.

- Use attachments for those who want more detail.

- Include in the body of the email:
   o what you need,
   o why you are asking (context),
   o in what format you need the information, and
   o by when.

- Offer to answer any questions and give times when you will be available and your preferred mode of response (call me [or email me] at…).

- Check punctuation and grammar. Email is a less formal mode of communication than in person or over the telephone, but when working across cultures, clarity and precision help the receiver understand the message.

- Read your message out loud (or have someone else read it) before you send it to make sure you did not miss anything you intended to include and to ensure the tone is acceptable, the grammar is correct, and the message is complete. This is especially important if you composed the email when in a negative state of emotion (such as anger or frustration).

- Never use email to start a disciplinary conversation. Use the telephone if you have to do this remotely.

Use the "out of office" feature in your email and provide specific information about who to contact in your absence.

USING VOICE MAIL

In remote teams, team members often have hours that do not overlap. It is likely that some of the communication will be left on voice mail. While team members seem to prefer to use email (you can get more information in an email and leave a data trail), it is more personal to use the telephone. When working globally after-hours, voice mail messages are typical. But even how the voice mail is set up and how available it is to callers can cause team problems.

Using Voice Mail

During a merger situation, human resources was considered an integral part of the team even though they were in a location remote to the rest of the team. The human resources team members each had published their office extension telephone numbers in the employee directory. In the directory they also published a general department number. The purpose of the department number was so that employees could call and leave a message when the individual members of the department were not available.

Impact on the Team

The other team members were more familiar with the general department number, so every time they called HR they got voice mail. The reputation of the human resources team suffered as they were seen as not readily available or accessible. Team members expressed disappointment with the lack of commitment on the part of the human resource members.

Any type of screening calls may give the impression that these members are not as interested in or available to other team members.

Here are some strategies for making the most out of any voice mail messages.

RECOMMENDED STRATEGIES FOR USING VOICE MAIL

General Strategies:

- With some forms of electronic equipment, such as video or telephone, there may be some distortion. To improve understanding of outgoing or incoming messages, pause for one second before starting to record a message. Speak clearly and just slightly more slowly than you might speak if in person.

Setting up voice mail:

- Pause before you speak to record your voice mail message. Speak clearly so callers can understand what you want them to do.

- Include what you are asking for (time of call, name, contact information, reason for the call, etc.).

For those with **Need for Certainty Orientation**:

Setting up voice mail:

- Use the "out of office" feature on the message when you will not be answering your telephone for extended periods, and provide specific information about who to call in your absence.

- Give callers information about who they can call if they need support now and you are not available.

Leaving a message:

- Be very specific. Include in the message:
  - who you are,
  - how you can be reached,
  - why you called,
  - when you called,
  - what you need, and
  - by when you need it.

- Give them information on how to reach you and when you will be available.

- Speak slowly and clearly (but not loudly).

- Repeat your name and telephone number again at the message's end, and do it slowly and distinctly.

BARRIERS TO EFFECTIVE COMMUNICATION

CAUSES OF COMMUNICATION BREAKDOWN

It does not take much for team members to become disillusioned with each other or with their team leader. Not only do communication failures negatively impact trust between team members, but they also slow down the work and often cause costly rework. Teams and team leaders who are effective at avoiding communication issues are more likely to achieve team outcomes on time.

Even a lack of clarity can create distrust and frustration.

Holding People Accountable

In a status update meeting, Sami raises a serious problem he has with the upstream department. He describes how their hand-offs to his department make project completion difficult. Sami's group needs to reformat and reconfigure the deliverables to complete their own responsibilities. This impedes progress for the line. Everyone leaves the meeting after a very productive problem-solving session. Three weeks later the same issue is raised by Sami since no changes have been made.

Impact on the Team

Team members are pointing fingers and avoiding taking responsibilities for their part of the solution. This team is very frustrated, and members are losing patience.

This team leader did not clarify what actual decision had been made about how to proceed. Nothing changed after the meeting because the team members were unclear whether the team leader had been discussing the solutions or had made a decision about the solution that was to be acted upon. The team leader was coached to do two things: 1) cut off the discussion once a decision had been made, and 2) be more explicit in the team meetings about when she was expressing an idea or an opinion and when she was making and announcing her decisions.

CLARIFYING THE PROJECT SCOPE

In the early stages of the team's work, it will be important to identify the Customer Acceptance Criteria (CAC) so the team knows the targets and outcomes. If the team leader engages the team members in collecting the data to define the CAC (Participative Orientation), it helps to keep the team members mindful of the outcomes required. In a more Hierarchical environment, senior staff will need to arrange for team members to gather data from people who are at higher levels in the organization than the team members. Senior executives can "open doors" for team members.

The CAC include all the features and functions of the "desired state" (also known as customer requirements). If it makes sense, construct a mock-up or draw pictures (consider screen shots). Talk with the customer about what the product or service will do. Ask the customer to:

- Describe what it (the outcome, the product, the service) might look like. Describe the final deliverable, such as what format the deliverable will take or what color it might come in.

- Describe how the final deliverable will be measured.

- Define specific criteria and requirements.

- Describe on what basis the outputs will be judged.

Meeting Customer Requirements

Ravi demonstrates the deliverables to the customer on time, but the solutions failed during the demonstration. This leaves the customer extremely dissatisfied and Ravi scrambling to explain what has gone wrong.

Impact on the Team

When Ravi meets with the team, members are pointing fingers at each sub-team (hardware and software) describing how their portion of the deliverable worked (so, therefore, it must be the other group who is at fault in the failure). Each sub-team has focused only on their deliverable and ignored that each portion needs to be able to work together in order to actually satisfy the customer.

Clarity on linkages as well as what is in scope (within the boundaries of the project) and out of scope also keeps the team focused on their deliverables, the needs of the project's customers, the customer requirements, and the end users of the outcomes of this project. The metaphor of a fence or any other boundary (such as a wall) is helpful in creating this visual. Within those boundaries are all the deliverables necessary to achieve the customer-defined outcomes.

Effective team leaders make sure their team members understand how the project deliverables align within the team as well as with the overall strategic initiatives of the organization.

The more team members understand the strategic alignment and financial implications, the more linked they will feel to the team and to the organization. They need to see how not having a scope definition, the schedule of milestone deliverables, and the budget allotted for this project can put the project at risk. The goal is to achieve the deliverables (scope) on time and under budget. Each member is more likely to succeed if they understand the role they play in achieving the desired outcome.

Often, it helps to link tasks to the roles of team members so they can visualize the handoffs and dependent variables (create a visual/flow chart to help those working in an acquired language). Tasks that need other tasks to be finished first are called dependent variables. For example, mailing out meeting invites is dependent on the task of creating the invitee list first.

In writing out the tasks for a project, make sure the team members understand the differences between a deliverable and a task. This table might be helpful.

Please note that the deliverables are typically nouns and describe the result of an activity while tasks start with a verb describing an activity.

DELIVERABLES	TASKS
Report	Write a report
A test environment	Test a system
Training materials	Train leaders
Menu of choices	Choose a system
Software documentation	Review a draft design
List of recommendations	Create a list for consideration

Effective team leaders understand how to drive towards achieving meeting results. They know how to get attendees actively and effectively involved in achieving outcomes. They focus both on process (what steps to take to work effectively), people (how to work together to accomplish outcomes), and content/outcomes (what needs to be accomplished).

BEFORE TEAM MEETINGS END

As the team meeting (or conference call) draws to a close, it is helpful to everyone if there is a brief recapitulation of what occurred in the meeting (Need for Certainty). This could include:

- What was decided

- What action items are outstanding

- Who the most responsible person is to handle each action item

- The expected date of completion

- Any items discussed but not finalized that should be added to future agendas

- Any items that were identified but not covered and should be added to future agendas

- A reminder to everyone of the date of the next scheduled meeting so they can put it in their calendars.

In acquired languages nuances are often lost. To avoid this, some leaders of multi-cultural teams hold post-meeting extension of the meeting to ensure that those who work in an acquired language truly understand meeting outcomes. This is a short opportunity (even when virtual) for each natural language group to spend five to ten minutes in their native language discussing what happened during the meeting. The team leader waits until each group has had their conversation, and he or she remains available to answer questions or clarify points before leaving the meeting space.

MEETING EVALUATION

Some team leaders, especially those with a Need for Certainty Orientation sometimes like to be sure that things have gone well in the meetings. One way they accomplish this is to evaluate the effectiveness of the team meeting by using a Plus/Delta approach.

Whether or not a meeting includes some critical or controversial scenarios, team leaders always can follow up with a team meeting evaluation. Conduct a Plus/Delta meeting evaluation to collect opinions on how the team members feel about how the meeting went (Participative Orientation). Of course with virtual teams this needs to be handled virtually or using a quick survey tool such as Survey Monkey (Individual Orientation). Alternatively, leaders can ask groups of people to discuss their answers and provide group responses to the Plus/Delta (Group Orientation).

To create a Plus/Delta format (with delta representing "change") see the sample below.

SAMPLE

DIRECTIONS:

In order to make sure we are focused on improving how the team works together, please take five minutes to fill out this form. In the left column please list those things about our meetings that are working well for you. You can also list things you want the team or team leader to keep doing (to repeat because they work well).

In the right column (the Delta column, which represents change) please focus on those things you see as opportunities for improvement and things you recommend be considered for change (what team members or the team leader could stop doing because it is not moving the team forward to achieve its deliverables). Once we collect your responses, this information will be shared anonymously. Please remember that we are asking for your input on how to improve team meetings and other team interactions.

Plus (+)	Delta (Δ)

_____END SAMPLE_____

A Plus/Delta evaluation is especially useful if the team leader shares the results with all team members after making sure no names or titles are used.

RECOMMENDED STRATEGIES FOR ESTABLISHING COMMUNICATION PROTOCOLS

For those with **Hierarchical Orientation:**

- The leader define the agenda and meeting report distribution list:
    - Who is on the distribution list and who gets copied (cc'ed)
    - How the names in the distribution set are listed (rank, alphabetical order, etc.)
    - How often status updates go to the team
    - What should be communicated regularly.

- The leader determines:
    - What should be included in voice mails (see above)
    - How should emails be structured and what should be included in emails (see above)
    - What is the agreed upon and expected response time for each kind of situation
    - How do you indicate when you need a response
    - How much context is expected (or is the agreed upon norm for the team).

- Start communications with an overview and executive summary then include more context and background (such as in an appendix).

- Check with people on status of decisions to be implemented and/or action items.

- Determine who needs to be informed but does not have to attend.

For those with <u>Need for Certainty Orientation</u>:

- Establish how often meetings should take place and at what time(s). Do not meet for meetings sake. Make sure there is a planned meeting outcome that is communicated.

- Explain your expectations for who should speak at meetings (e.g., will you use a roll call system?).

- Provide a written agenda in advance.

- Send other meeting materials to attendees in advance to allow time to review.

- Create agendas and invitations with the time stamp of each location.

- Notify in advance those people whom you want to speak or present to give them enough time to prepare.

- Include time frames on the agenda for each presenter and adhere to them (NOTE: Give them more time if English is an acquired language).

- Poll the team members and ask everyone's opinion (but allow them to "pass").

- If you want to use the mute button:
    o Get permission to go on mute for a specified period of time
    o Take the time for your conversation
    o When you come back, say thank you to others and explain what was covered.

- Include timelines and clear deliverables.

- Provide written text and visuals to illustrate your message.

- Determine when to distribute meeting notes and status updates.

- Prepare and distribute written minutes after the meeting with action items, responsible parties, and due dates.

- Record outcomes and minutes and send them in writing.

- Resolve any meeting issues.

For those with <u>Group Orientation</u>:

- Provide short bios with work and personal data that participants supply.

For those with <u>Quality of Life Orientation</u>:

- Periodically check that everyone is still on the call.

- In your written communications, use sub-headings to clarify new topics to make it easier for others to follow the way you organized the content.

- Determine if there are any conflicts between people that couldn't be resolved during the meeting
    o Minimize the escalation of any action items or issues
    o Determine the time frame for notes to be distributed.

NOTE: How conflicts are resolved are an aspect of Achievement/Quality of Life Orientations.

For those with <u>Achievement Orientation</u>:

- Decide on appropriate response times.

- Reserve time at the beginning and end of the meeting for technology setup and break down.

SPECIFIC ASPECTS OF THE CULTURAL ORIENTATIONS NAMED IN THIS CHAPTER

Need for Certainty Orientation	There are formal and widely understood ways of behaving and getting the work done; there is comfort in structured situations; invest up front in analysis, guidance, and/or information; provide full and complete information and context.
Group Orientation	Relationships prevail over tasks; teams get rewarded together and recognition goes to the group as a whole; opinions are predetermined by group membership; make the case for common interests and what is for the benefit of the group (team or company).
Hierarchical Orientation	Hierarchy in organizations reflects existential inequality between higher and lower levels; employees expect to be told what to do; it is the leader's responsibility to make things happen.
Individualism Orientation	Everyone is expected to have a private opinion. Speaking one's mind is a characteristic of an honest person.
Participative Orientation	Subordinates expect to be consulted; good ideas and suggestions can come from any organizational level; inequality should be minimized.
Quality of Life Orientation	Helping others is valued.
Achievement Orientation	Assertiveness and competitiveness are valued.

important

Chapter 12
Building Trust and Relationships

Research (Watson Wyatt 2002) indicates that organizations with a high level of trust outperform organizations with low trust by nearly three times. This research also shows that it was trust on the teams within those organizations that allowed the organizations to outperform their competitors.

Trust between a team leader and members and among team members has both logical and emotional components. This chapter will explore the logical (cognitive, "what I think") and emotional (affective, "how I feel") aspects of trust.

Trust on teams is based on assumptions as to how team members will perform on some future occasion, and these assumptions are based on past behavior. Trusting assumes that those who are trusted will not take advantage of the openness and vulnerability created by the person who trusts. Trust implies an expectation by the person who trusts that the other(s) will behave in a predictable and open manner.

In situations where the team members do not know each other or do not know the team leader, there is an element of risk in trusting. In new situations, vulnerability is greater. If one chooses to trust and that trust is abused, there may be a more negative reaction, higher potential for regretting the decision to trust, and an increased reluctance to trust others in future new situations.

Building trust needs to start early in the life of the team. Otherwise team members may build up distrust without consciously realizing what is happening. It is important to note that some people innately trust others until something is done to break that trust, while others are skeptical and expect people to earn their trust.

In Group-Oriented cultures it is more likely that people will trust those of their in-group and less likely to trust those not part of the in-groups (or at least expect them to have to prove they are worthy of trust first).

BUILDING TRUST

Trust is one of the most important factors underlying effective working relationships. Successful teams require members (and leaders) to behave toward each other in ways that justify and enhance mutual trust. They do not abuse the information they gain, nor do they undermine each other. In its simplest form, trust in team relationships is the belief that a person's word is reliable and that each person will fulfill his or her obligation in any work or personal interaction.

RECOMMENDED STRATEGIES FOR BUILDING TRUST

For those with Group Orientation:

- Prove you are willing to trust by demonstrating your level of investment in the relationships.

- Demonstrate your commitment to the project (team outcomes) and the people on the team.

- Communicate with team members often, both in and outside team meetings.

- Focus on shared goals (rather than personal goals).

- Even if the other is perceived as "impossible to work with," focus on the team outcomes, not the person. You do not have to like your team members, but the team does need to achieve its stated outcomes and work towards that common goal.

For those with Achievement Orientation:

- Keep your commitments and promises.

For those with Tolerance for Ambiguity Orientation:

- Tell the truth even when it may expose your own error.

- Share information—more than is requested. Provide this in summaries with backup supporting documents so that those who need less can read the summaries.

- Be open-minded about "how to do things." There are many ways to get things done; your way may not be the best. Listen openly to what others consider best approaches.

- Let others do it their way when it is not your responsibility.

For those with <u>Participative Orientation</u>:

- Treat others as equals. While they may not have the same skills or skill levels you have, they may have other complementary skills. Assume they are bringing something valuable to the team.

Note: This also is appropriate for those with Tolerance for Ambiguity Orientation.

For those with <u>Individual Orientation</u>:

- Act and speak consistently.

For those with <u>Quality of Life Orientation</u>:

- Do what's right rather than just doing the right things.

BUILDING COGNITIVE TRUST

Cognitive trust is knowledge-driven; it is based on the results of rational thought, such as predictable performance outcomes, rather than emotions. Cognitive trust (predictability or reliability) is based on knowledge that has been accumulated from observations and from the reputation of others based on how they have carried out their previous work.

Those with Need for Certainty and Achievement Orientations are more likely to use cognitive approaches to trusting others.

RECOMMENDED STRATEGIES FOR BUILDING COGNITIVE TRUST

For those with a mix of **Individual**, **Achievement** and **Need for Certainty Orientations**:

- Share information about your skills and capabilities.

- Endorse the skills and value that each member brings to the team.

- Provide a clear team purpose and vision.

- Do what you say you will do (DWYSYWD).

- Create an "Operating Agreement" with the team.

Barriers to cognitive trust include what is perceived as:

- Lack of response "in time."

- Lack of information / incomplete information—hoarding.

- Broken task commitments.

- Rejection of ideas, approaches, perspectives of others.

- Lack of respect (for me, my position/expertise, my time, my deliverables, my commitments, my clients, my line manager).

- Failure to tell the truth (avoids bad news).

- Lack of communication / not available.

BUILDING AFFECTIVE TRUST

Affective trust is based on the level of genuine concern and care each team member or leader demonstrates to others. Affective trust is based on feelings and on personal experiences rather than knowledge about the reputation of the other. Those with Group-Orientated or Quality of Life leanings are more likely to rely on affective trust.

RECOMMENDED STRATEGIES FOR BUILDING AFFECTIVE TRUST

For those with a mix of <u>Quality of Life, Participative</u>, and <u>Group Orientation</u>:

- Personalize e-mails; avoid e-mail blasts.

- Have regular one-to-one conversations with each other.

- Pay attention to news items from your other locations; talk about global current events.

- Learn about each member's culture and flex your approach.

- Learn about each member's communication preferences and use them. Recognize and reward team member contributions based on their cultural preference. For example, in some cultures individual rewards are considered embarrassing.

Barriers to affective trust include what is perceived as:

- Lack of personalization of responses to others.

- Broken commitments to the group.

- Consistent rejection of the ideas of others and an unwillingness to listen to different approaches.

- Lack of personal interactions (does not greet people; gets right down to business; cares more about the task than the people).

- Does not understand (or tolerate) when others have personal challenges that may affect project work.

MEASURING TRUST

If there appears to be a lack of trust among and between team members, it might help to use an activity to measure the level of trust. A more formal approach emphasizes the serious nature of the activity.

Conduct a paper and pencil objective or on-line assessment of trust regarding:

- The level of expertise (of other team members).

- The level of capability.

- The level of performance (or previous performance).

- The reputation.

- The level of integrity.

- The level of effective human process interactions between team members. (This can be measured using the Global Team Process Questionnaire™ system. See Chapter 22 for more information on this instrument.)

- The previous track records.

- The ability of other team members to conduct a thorough and careful analysis of the situation.

- Level of caution vs. risk.

- The level of caring responses.

- The level of warm and caring attitude.

- Willingness to listen.

teach this as necessary

- The level of effective listening.

This will identify areas that need team leader (or consultant) attention. See Chapter 18 for an instructor guide on building trust and relationships and resolving trust issues.

DEMONSTRATING TRUST

Here are some strategies for team leaders and team members to demonstrate they are trustworthy and that they want to build relationships with other team members.

RECOMMENDED STRATEGIES FOR DEMONSTRATING TRUST

For those with <u>Hierarchical Orientation</u>:

- Leaders can show loyalty by acting as a buffer between what happens outside the team and team members.

For those with <u>Group Orientation</u>:

- Be loyal. Leaders and members can show loyalty by championing the work of the team and of other team members (for example, talking about the effective work of others to people outside the team).

For those with <u>Quality of Life Orientation</u>:

- Say thank you.

- Focus on helping others learn from mistakes rather than reacting negatively.

- Show respect for others even when they disagree with you (or you disagree with them).

- Set a good example. Conduct yourself in a manner that demonstrates how you want team members to treat each other.

- Be a buffer between the team and outsiders by speaking up for the team and the team members.

- Catch the team members doing something right and recognize them for it.

For those with <u>Achievement and Short-term Orientation</u>:

- Mention work done well (on time, quick thinking, under budget, when savings or efficiencies are introduced, quality, going above and beyond, working long hours, etc.).

positive reinforcement

For those with <u>Individual and Achievement Orientation</u>:

- Show you are confident when warranted.

For those with <u>Participative Orientation</u>:

- Leaders, do not ask your team members to do anything you will not do.

BUILDING RAPPORT

Building rapport (finding out what you have in common) can help build trust. It might help teams to remember that regardless of how someone goes about getting their job done as a team member, all of them are committed to achieving the team results (common ground). Differences are only different ways of getting at the same outcome.

In science-based, financial and other industries with significant regulatory requirements, there is a strong Need for Certainty due to the rules or parameters defined by law or policy.

Takes leader skill to do this!

Building Rapport

A pharmaceutical biostatistics and clinical programming department had each department member define their "lifeline" (a description of important events in their life). They were given specific rules within which to work (Need for Certainty) and were asked only to reveal that which they were willing to share with others on the team.

Outcomes

During the sharing part of the activity, a lot of common ground was shared in areas such as educational background, relocation experiences, and work experiences. Some very touching and personal incidents were found to be shared by members of the pairs. This helped the team members recognize specific things they had in common. Attendees expressed how much being able to learn about each other helped them understand the paths each of them had taken to become members of the team.

In addition to the work, there are lots of intersections that team members have in common. It will help build rapport between team members if leaders tease this out for them. Encourage them to talk about topics such as music, theater or movies, books, cultural events, etc.

BUILDING RAPPORT TO HELP DEVELOP RELATIONSHIPS

People who are task-driven (Individual or Achievement Orientations) may be perceived by those preferring to have relationships with those in working groups (Group or Quality of Life Orientation) as cold, uncaring, task-focused, and difficult to trust. For these types, building relationships seems to be a waste of time and "gets in the way of getting the job done." They do not seem to need personal communications, except those related directly to tasks, to get work accomplished.

For others with Group and Quality of Life Orientations, personal relationships and caring for others are a key to trust, which in turn is necessary for accomplishing tasks. Since there are often both types in teams, there needs to be some relationship building activities as well as activities devoted to task accomplishment. Effective team leaders recognize the need for both approaches and can easily explain why team building or relationship building activities are important to the success of the whole team.

To help establish relationships, people need to know a bit about each other personally, other than tasks and capabilities. Here are some strategies to try to help team members (whether meeting virtually or face-to-face) build relationships with each other.

RECOMMENDED STRATEGIES FOR BUILDING RAPPORT

For those with <u>Group Orientation</u>:

- Encourage team members to communicate with each other outside team meetings (voice contact is better at building relationships than email).

For those with <u>Hierarchical Orientation</u>:

- Leaders may need to "give team members permission" to speak with each other by telephone outside team meetings (the telephone is better at building relationships than email, and those with a Hierarchical Orientation need to be given this "permission" by the leader).

Here are some general recommendations on building rapport:

- Notice the pace of speech of the team members. When conversing with them and when asking them questions, you may wish to slow down your speech (and avoid jargon) to help the comprehension of those who speak a different primary language.

- Ask open-ended questions to get others involved in the conversation.

- Offer to help. ("That seems like you are asking for some support. How can I help? What do you need from me in order to help you to make this deadline?")

- Listen carefully and listen for meaning (what they mean, not just what they say).

- Do not interrupt even when there is silence. Some cultures are "cultures of silence" (i.e., they have longer pauses between thoughts or sentences). Also, it may be necessary for team members to gather their thoughts before speaking. Give them time. If the period of silence gets quite long, ask if they need time to think about their answer and offer to come back to them after you let someone else speak. (Do not forget to go back to them.)

- Help establish norms to avoid having team members interrupting others, finishing sentences started by others, or "explaining" what other team members have said ("I think what John means is...").

- Use communication techniques to show that you understand or care to know more. Here are some examples:
  - I can follow that logic.
  - Please say more about that.
  - Does that mean...?
  - I see what you mean.
  - That sound like it is a difficult situation.

To build rapport you can also:

- Show respect through use of honorifics appropriate for their culture such as Herr Doktor Professor (Germany), allowing for silence (Asian cultures), etc. This is especially expected by the older generations.

- Find commonalities; ask them about their favorite food, books, movies, music, etc.

- Be sociable. Talk about social things or news items, not only work activities.

- Act in ways to build relationships between team members such as using icebreakers, socializing, and/or successes since the group spoke previously.

- Share your background (education, other successful team work, lessons learned on other teams, special capabilities, specific issues, help or support needed...)
  - Say: What I want to learn is...
  - Ask: Who can help me gain access to...

- Focus on both people and their work.

- Create "high social presence." The use of social media may work well with the younger generation.

SPECIFIC ASPECTS OF THE CULTURAL ORIENTATIONS NAMED IN THIS CHAPTER

Group Orientation	Relationships prevail over tasks.
Quality of Life Orientation	Modesty, solidarity, and helping others are virtues. Excellence is something one keeps to oneself; it easily leads to jealousy.
Need for Certainty Orientation	There is comfort in structured situations; managers are expected to have the answers.
Participative Orientation	Inequalities among people should be minimized. Subordinates expect to be consulted.
Tolerance for Ambiguity Orientation	Resolution of conflicts by compromise and negotiation.
Achievement Orientation	Good managers should be assertive and decisive. A performance society is ideal; support for the strong. Assertiveness, competitiveness and ambition are virtues. Resolution of conflicts by a show of strength or by fighting.
Hierarchical Orientation	Work tasks are clearly presented; employees are expected to be told what to do. Work gets done most efficiently when appropriate channels are used; employees rely more on their managers for direction.

Chapter 13
Working Across Cultures

Cultural dimensions offer a framework, a starting point from which to analyze the behaviors of others. Developing the ability to recognize behaviors that indicate a preference for one orientation or the other can build one's cultural repertoire and increase intercultural competence.

When talking about culture, it is easy to focus on the research and theories. It is not so easy to convey the advantages or relative benefits of one cultural orientation over another, especially when balancing the belief that neither is right or wrong—they are just different.

People who want practical application of theories ask, "So what?" While this book offers many strategies to consider and suggests the cultural orientations with which they align best, the information below is designed to bring the importance of cultural competence and the relative benefits of each cultural orientation into greater focus. In addition to the application of cultural knowledge to teams, the examples below offer a broader application of how to build your cultural repertoire.

Hofstede offers the example on the following page of how the dimensions might impact the negotiations process.

One cultural orientation is not any better than another. Each has its advantages. The following tables show the relative advantages of the various orientations discussed in previous chapters and provide examples of strategies that can be used when working or managing in a multi-cultural environment.

Negotiating Across Cultures: How the Dimensions Affect the Negotiations Process

- *Individualism* – "...will affect the need for stable relationships between (opposing) negotiators. In a collectivist culture replacement of a person means that a new relationship will have to be built, which takes time. Mediators (go-betweens) are key in maintaining a viable pattern of relationships that allows progress."

- *Power Distance* – "...will affect the degree of centralization of the control and decision-making structure and the importance of the status of the negotiators."

- *Certainty* – "...will affect the (in)tolerance of ambiguity and (dis)trust in opponents who show unfamiliar behaviors, as well as the need for structure and ritual in the negotiation procedures."

- *Achievement* – "...will affect the need for ego-boosting behavior and the sympathy for the strong on the part of negotiators and their superiors, as well as the tendency to resolve conflicts by a show of force. Feminine cultures are more likely to resolve conflicts by compromise and to strive for consensus."

- *Time Orientation* – "...will affect the perseverance to achieve desired ends even at the cost of sacrifices."[6]

RECOMMENDED STRATEGIES FOR WORKING ACROSS CULTURES

For those with Individual Orientation:

- Appeal to their self-interest.

- Focus on how the results or the change will be good for them individually.

- Allow individual work and competition between individuals.

- Delegate to individuals.

[6] Geert Hofstede, Cultures and Organizations: Software of the Mind, 3rd edition, p. 400

- Allow individuals to formulate and ask questions before and during the work.

- Provide feedback, recognition, and rewards to individuals.

- Decisions can be made quickly by individuals whose role or position enables them to speak on behalf of the larger group.

- Recognize that task completion will often take precedence over establishing and maintaining relationships.

- Recognize that colleagues will not feel the need to consult others before making a decision.

- Learn to expect direct and quick answers to your questions.

- Allow individual work.

- Stress individual capabilities and expertise.

For those with Group Orientation:

- Appeal to the common interest.

- Focus on how the results or changes will be good for the group.

- Work with team/partnering approaches—small groups with reporting to the larger group. Allow colleagues to consult with each other without being suspicious about it.

- Delegate to groups or teams.

- Allow the group discussion to formulate and ask questions as well as to consult with each other and spend time working out their responses, questions, and concerns.

- Provide feedback, recognition, and rewards to groups.

- Decisions are generally reached by consensus; resistance is likely if you do not allow time for this to occur.

- Recognize that establishing and maintaining relationships takes precedence over task completion.

- Allow colleagues to consult with each other and spend time working out their responses, questions, and concerns.

- Learn not to expect direct and quick answers to your questions.

- Foster a team/collaborative or partnering approach.

- Focus on the capabilities of the team.

For those with <u>Hierarchical Orientation</u>:

- Leverage the "power position" of senior management to:
  - o Drive the projects.
  - o Make introductions and connections.
  - o Delegate deliverables.
  - o Communicate expectations.
  - o Provide status updates.

- Use legitimate power (management or seniority) to exercise authority.

- Use an approach with higher-ups that is perceived as a "help me understand" posture.

- When dealing with change, tell subordinates what to do differently. Do not leave it to them to figure out "how" to do things differently.

- Use "expert power" (your credibility and facts) to exercise authority.

- Use the proper organizational channels. Respect the formality of the hierarchy.

For those with <u>Participative Orientation</u>:

- Include stakeholders at all levels in self-directed discussions.
  - o Provide them with choices to discuss.
  - o Explain your position and suggestions.
  - o Ask for their input and perspectives.
  - o Allow for questions and challenges.

- Use more gentle persuasion and influencing skills with those at all levels.

- With higher-ups, demonstrate initiative and problem-solving skills.

- When dealing with change, provide a forum where people can be involved in discussion and framing "how" things will be different (work processes during the interim) after you provide the "what."

- Use influencing skills with superiors, peers, and direct reports.

- Expect and allow employees to go to the right sources regardless of their position in the hierarchy.

For those with <u>Certainty Orientation</u>:

- Focus on compliance with procedures and policies.

- Provide specific rules and structures/interim structures.

- Use tools to provide analysis—for example, to help others see the cost-benefit comparison.

- Anticipate the information they will need. Have available lots of supporting data and even theory, if appropriate. Use a logical flow to your interactions.

- Provide opportunities to answer questions (and preempt questions that should be asked).

- Provide them with examples of others who have used the approach successfully.

- Use a logical flow to your interactions. Describe the logic.

For those with <u>Tolerance for Ambiguity Orientation</u>:

- Focus on improvement rather than accepting the status quo.

- Challenge and question "the way things are done" while offering alternatives for their consideration.

- Reward creative behavior that moves the group/division/company toward the end even if it was "outside the box."

- Share information and open many communication forums.

- Provide them with an outline of information to use in decision-making. They may not need to know how it is going to work as long as the numbers make sense.

- There is less need to prove others have tried an approach and that it works, although a case study couldn't hurt (but provide it in bullets).

- Focus on creativity and allowing time and interactions to flex as necessary.

For those with <u>Tolerance for Achievement Orientation</u>:

- Stress and reward performance, getting work done on time or early.

- Show drive and ambition for completion of tasks and meeting deadlines.

- Communicate and respond with a sense of urgency.

- A good colleague and a good manager should be decisive.

- Resolve conflicts with a show of strength.

- Deliver what you promise, when you promise, and give more than you promised.

- Expect that work may take precedence over family life.

For those with Tolerance for Quality of Life Orientation:

- Stress solidarity and service.

- Emphasize humility and modesty in your approach.

- Recognize quality may be more important than quantity or speed.

- A good colleague and a good manager should be intuitive.

- Resolve conflicts by compromise and negotiation.

- Focus on continued service to the internal and external customer.

- Remember that employees have a family life and take this into account.

For those with Long-Term Orientation:

- Define success over a long time horizon.

- Show patience and perseverance.

- Expect business loyalties to remain stable over time.

- Stress the importance of mid/long-term benefits.

- Be willing to adapt policies and guidelines to different contexts.

- Provide rewards consistently, based on regular patterns.

- Define success over a long time horizon.

- Allow managers time and resources to make their own contributions.

- Invest in future outcomes.

- Be willing to adapt policies and guidelines to different contexts.

- Understanding is seen as a long process that requires considerable mental effort.

- Learners prefer a slow, accurate, systematic approach. Memorization is a way to deepen understanding.

- For learners, use clear delineation of concepts. Reinforce use of processes with repetitive practice.

For those with Short-Term Orientation:

- Plan to achieve quick results and rapidly fulfill business priorities.

- Be willing to accelerate the pace of negotiation and decision making.

- Expect that business loyalties change over time.

- Stress the importance of immediate benefits.

- Apply the same policies and guidelines widely whatever the context.

- Provide variable rewards based on achievement of results.

- Focus on immediate transactional success.

- Set expectations for rapid fulfillment of business priorities.

- Set expectations for current outcomes.

- Apply the same policies and guidelines widely whatever the context.

- Understanding is seen as a process of sudden insight.

- Learners prefer an approach which incorporates investigative and analytical thinking. Use questioning and probing, and encourage learners to prove intellectual points by using logical arguments.

- For learners, use abstract thinking and open discussions.

For those with Indulgence Orientation:

- Demonstrate a positive attitude.

- Exuberance and optimism are valued.

- In customer service positions and the public realm in general, smiling is expected.

- Happiness and a sense of well-being are important.

For those with Restraint Orientation:

- Demonstrate a sober, serious demeanor.

- Caution and circumspection are valued.

- In customer service positions and the public realm in general, smiling is suspect. Rather, a stern face is a sign of seriousness.

- Self-control is important.

Many Cultures, One Team Activities

In order to help consultants, human resources professionals and team leaders use some of the ideas in the previous sections of this book, Part III includes "Instructor Guides" for activities, some of which were previously mentioned. Some are applicable for co-located teams or virtual teams.

Some instructor guides are designed for use with an in-person meeting. Some have options for how to use with in-person meetings or virtual ones.

Chapter 14
Blunders in International Business Activity

You can create a game to help people (in an enjoyable way) see how pervasive culture is and how easy it is to make a cultural gaff. The puzzle pieces can be customized to focus on specific functional areas such as marketing or HR. The pieces provided here are from a lot of different examples from various functional areas. In addition to the clients as a source, you can use David Ricks' book *Blunders in International Business* for ideas.

You can use the information gathered or researched to create a simple game where each person receives one or two puzzle pieces. (I usually set them out with the participant materials.)

After the facilitator explains the game, each person walks around the room to find the other piece of their puzzle (each puzzle is only two pieces). When everyone has found their partner (the person with the piece that fits together with theirs), they each read their puzzle piece starting with the partner who has the top of the puzzle (straight cut on top) and then the other person reads the "punch line" or the bottom of the puzzle.)

After all pieces have been read, the facilitator asks a series of questions about what they learned about culture in hearing the cultural blunders. I am including some examples here, as well as facilitation questions, so you can create your own materials and games.

At the end of the activity, participants will be able to:
- Comment on how wide-spread the impact of culture is.
- Provide several examples from the simulation of the impact of culture.
- Describe why it is important to attend to cultural differences.
- Admit that it is very easy to make a cultural blunder.

TIMING

Activity Instructions	2 minutes
Activity	10 - 18 minutes
Debrief	20 - 30 minutes

DURING THE ACTIVITY

Do: Explain the activity to the participants.

If you have one puzzle for each person, this would be two non-matching pieces at the start of the activity, say: *This activity is called "Blunders in International Business." In this activity you are going to have to get up and walk around with your puzzle pieces. Each completed puzzle will contain one blunder. Each puzzle is made up of only two pieces. Someone in the room has the other piece of your puzzle. Your task is to assemble a complete puzzle. When you are finished, you each should have at least one puzzle that looks like mine.*

Do: Hold up a completed puzzle for them to see.

If you have only one puzzle piece for each person, say:

This activity is called "Blunders in International Business." In this activity you are going to have to get up and walk around with your puzzle pieces. Each completed puzzle contains one blunder. Each puzzle is made up of only two pieces. Someone in the room has the other piece of your puzzle. Your task is to find your partner, who has the piece that will complete your puzzle. When you find your partner, please stand together until everyone has found their partner and completed all the puzzles. When it is complete, it will look like this.

Do: Hold up a completed puzzle for them to see.

Ask: *Are there any questions?*

Say: *You may begin.*

Do: Watch them, and when everyone finds a full puzzle or their partner...

DEBRIEF THE ACTIVITY

Say: *Now I would to like each of you to read you puzzle(s) or piece.*

Do: Model what you want by them to do by reading your puzzle pieces slowly and distinctly. Have each participant read from their puzzle. Let them comment, laugh, etc. You may need to explain the puzzles if your participants are working in an acquired language.

Ask: *What does culture impact? Give me some examples from this activity.*

Expected Responses:

(These will depend on which puzzles you include)

- Colors
- Greetings
- Flowers
- Work activities
- Names of products
- Etc.

Ask: Do any of you have any examples of blunders from your own experience that you would like to share?

Do: Listen to those who share.

Ask: What were some of the lessons you learned from this activity that you can take with you after this session?

Expected Responses:

(Answers will vary)

- Culture touches everything.
- It is easy to make a cultural blunder.
- It might be helpful to get some cultural training.
- It might be helpful to have a culture mentor.
- I wish I had known this before...

NOTES ON CREATING PUZZLE PIECES

To create game pieces:

- Write out your "puzzle" examples.

    - Sample 1: (TOP PUZZLE PIECE) Coke introduces the product Fresca to Mexico... (BOTTOM PUZZLE PIECE)...where a "Fresca" means "lesbian."
    - Sample 2: (TOP PUZZLE PIECE) An ad, "**When** I used this shirt, I felt good..." (BOTTOM PUZZLE PIECE)... translated into Spanish as, "**Until** I used this shirt, I felt good."
    - Sample 3: (TOP PUZZLE PIECE) McDonald's uses Hispanic ads in Puerto Rico... (BOTTOM PUZZLE PIECE)...where they were unsuccessful because they were considered "too Mexican."

- o Sample 4: (TOP PUZZLE PIECE) Volvo promotional tactics vary...(BOTTOM PUZZLE PIECE)...in the US they promote economy, durability, and safety; in Mexico, price; in Venezuela, quality.
- o Sample 5: (TOP PUZZLE PIECE) The Regional VP sent a thank-you of yellow flowers to a Hispanic client...(BOTTOM PUZZLE PIECE)...yellow flowers represent death/disrespect in Mexico.
- o Sample 6: (TOP PUZZLE PIECE) On April 2nd, 2013, a Regional VP corrected a Costa Rican manager for missing a 3/12/13 contract deadline...(BOTTOM PUZZLE PIECE)...3/12/13 is December 3, 2013 outside the US.
- o Sample 7: (TOP PUZZLE PIECE) A US manager gave his Chinese employee a poor rating for not participating in meetings...(BOTTOM PUZZLE PIECE)...the employee was trying to be polite, so he waited for silence (to indicate others were finished) before offering his opinion.

- Put two of the "puzzles" on a page in about 32 or 36 point type (see sample below).

  - o It may be easier if you put them into table boxes (one at the top and one at the bottom of the page. This will give you some guidelines for cutting the puzzle pieces into two puzzles.
  - o Center them from top to bottom and leave room between the two puzzles as well as the top and bottom of each puzzle.
  - o Print off the one copy of the pages using various colors of paper. Color paper makes it easier for the users to find the other half of their puzzle.

> A manager was criticized by a director who saw the manager repeatedly touching a potential client...
>
> ...touching is very natural (and expected) in Hispanic cultures.

> When offered a cup of Cuban coffee the senior executive said, "No thanks, your coffee is too strong for me..."
>
> ...this was considered rude. Drinking coffee and having conversation is a Cuban experience with strong cultural roots

- Laminate each page.

- Cut the page in half on the straight line across the center. (You now have a set of puzzles, each with one cultural example on it. You will notice that there is a space between the first part of the statement (which ends in an ellipsis) and the second part (starts with an ellipsis).

- Now take each puzzle and make any **not straight** cut across between the top and the bottom part of the "puzzle." You can use any kind of curvy or straight lines as long as they all are different. The crazier the better...

Chapter 15

Cultural Blunders Mix and Match Activity

For those situations where the team is virtual, this game is similar to the previous activity but in the form of a "mix and matching" test.

PREPARATION CHECKLIST

The only preparation for this activity is to send out the materials in advance of the video or teleconference and ask attendees to bring a copy to the meeting. You can start the meeting with this as an icebreaker.

TIMING

Activity Set-up and Explanation	2 minutes	
Activity	5 – 10 minutes	
Debrief	10 minutes	

DURING THE ACTIVITY

Do: Explain the activity to the participants.

Say: *This is an activity intended to give a few examples of blunders that others have made while doing business internationally. You are to read the start of the sentences in the left column and try to match the end of the statement with only one of the statements in the right column. You have five minutes to make your choices.*

Ask: Are there any questions?

DEBRIEF THE ACTIVITY

Do: (at five minutes or earlier if they all seem to have finished). Review the correct answers using your answer key.

Ask: *Do any of you have any examples of cultural blunders that you have experienced or that you know about that you care to share with the group?*

Do: Allow them to share their experiences.

Ask: *Why do you think this activity is relevant to the work we are doing together?*

Expected Responses:

- Because we are a multi-cultural group.

- Because culture touches all we do.

- Because culture may interfere with our being able to work well together if we do not understand each other better.

Do: Repeat or add any other purpose that is relevant to the work of your group. Make the transition into the next activity or work process.

HANDOUT

Directions: When matched correctly, the phrases on the following page describe cultural blunders. See if you can match the phrases by placing the appropriate letter from the right column in the appropriate box in the left column.

1. ___ On April 1st, 2005, an RVP scolded a Costa Rican broker for missing a 3/12/05 contract deadline...

2. ___ An American team leader always held his team meetings on Thursday at 2 PM...

3. ___ The French bid submission was over 1" thick; the US was only ten pages...

4. ___ McDonalds spent years in litigation in France...

5. ___ France set up a timber mill in Africa...

6. ___ The OK gesture...

7. ___ The US manager sent her Chinese counterparts December holiday greeting cards in red envelopes...

8. ___ A French manager in a global company organized with matrix reporting relationships wanted to please his supervisors...

9. ___ A French executive was a little perturbed when an American colleague asked him what he did over the weekend...

10. ___ An employee from Hong Kong was quite distressed...

11. ___ An American became annoyed when his European counterpart did not respond to his emailed questions...

12. ___ A Franco-American joint venture recognized that cultural differences were a problem...

A. ...the Chinese were disappointed to find only a holiday greeting card in the envelope. Red envelopes are used to give bonuses.

B. ...when a French colleague kissed her hello and goodbye when he came to the Hong Kong office.

C. ...means "zero" in France.

D. ...over partners' attitudes about cleanliness.

E. ...3/12/05 is December 3, 2005, in many non-US countries.

F. ...only after eight years of ineffective collaboration.

G. ...in India it is 12:30 AM
...in China it is 3 AM
...in France it is 8 PM

H. ...the company selected the French proposal because it had more context and background.

I. ...but was unsure which boss, the global franchise leader or the local operations leader, really had the most power.

J. ...the European was annoyed that the American did not care enough about the work to pick up the telephone when he had a question or needed an answer.

K. ...where there was not enough power to run the mill.

L. ...some French see a distinct separation between their professional life and their personal life and see this kind of question as an intrusion.

answers next page ⟶

HANDOUT ANSWER KEY

Directions: When matched correctly, the phrases below describe cultural blunders. See if you can match the phrases by placing the appropriate letter from the right column in the appropriate box in the left column.

E On April 1st, 2005, an RVP scolded a Costa Rican broker for missing a 3/12/05 contract deadline…

E. …3/12/05 is December 3, 2005, in many non-US countries.

G An American team leader always held his team meetings on Thursday at 2 PM…

G. …in India it is 12:30 AM
…in China it is 3 AM
…in France it is 8 PM

H The French bid submission was over 1" thick; the US was only ten pages…

H. …the company selected the French proposal because it had more context and background.

D McDonalds spent years in litigation in France…

D. …over partners' attitudes about cleanliness.

K France set up a timber mill in Africa…

K. …where there was not enough power to run the mill.

C The OK gesture… What's ?

C. …means "zero" in France.

A The US manager sent her Chinese counterparts December holiday greeting cards in red envelopes…

A. …the Chinese were disappointed to find only a holiday greeting card in the envelope. Red envelopes are used to give bonuses.

I A French manager in a global company organized with matrix reporting relationships wanted to please his supervisors…

I. …but was unsure which boss, the global franchise leader or the local operations leader, really had the most power.

L A French executive was a little perturbed when an American colleague asked him what he did over the weekend…

L. …some French see a distinct separation between their professional life and their personal life and see this kind of question as an intrusion.

B An employee from Hong Kong was quite distressed…

B. …when a French colleague kissed her hello and goodbye when he came to the Hong Kong office.

J An American became annoyed when his European counterpart did not respond to his emailed questions…

J. …the European was annoyed that the American did not care enough about the work to pick up the telephone when he had a question or needed an answer.

F A Franco-American joint venture recognized that cultural differences were a problem…

F. …only after eight years of ineffective collaboration.

Chapter 16
Cultural Diversity Activity

Cultural metacognition refers to a person's reflective thinking about his or her cultural assumptions. Understanding and leveraging of multiculturalism will be the next competitive advantage for global companies and those that do business with diverse customers.

Cultural differences (foundational values) impact everything. Training is not exportable globally without revisions or redesign. This means aligning the methodology used in learning with the cultural orientations of the attendees needs. For example:

- Brainstorming is more likely to be effective as an Individual and Achievement Orientation type of activity.

- Small group work is a preferred Group and Participative Orientation type of activity.

- Lecture is more expected as a Hierarchical Orientation type of activity.

Cultural differences can be measured and taken into account (training, managing others, working in teams, leading, marketing, customer support, etc.).

This activity is designed to help participants recognize how diverse people are in what we like to do, what we eat, and how we work. The activity can be accomplished with a group of at least ten or groups in the hundreds (for this large-size you will need a microphone!).

This is an activity that requires participants to make forced choices about what they prefer. You can add or subtract any forced choice items from list provided and/or alter it to include tasks that the session participants do in their daily work. For example:

1) a forced choice for trainers might be DESIGN or DELIVER;

2) a forced choice for the finance function might be TRACK THE NUMBERS (analysis of the actual numbers) or SCENARIO PLANNING (analysis of what *might* happen in the future).

At the end of the module, participants will be able to:

- Comment on how widespread issues of diversity are.

- Identify that even their friends have preferences different from theirs.

177

- Recognize that culturally diverse groups of people do not all have similar preferences.

- Describe what surprised them about their preferences and the preferences of others.

Audience: Co-located teams or a meeting with everyone present.

PREPARATION CHECKLIST

There is no particular preparation needed for this activity except reviewing the activity directions and points for debrief.

TIMING

	Activity Set-up and Explanation	5 minutes
	Activity	15 minutes
	Debrief	10 minutes

DURING THE ACTIVITY

Left/Right—Used with interchangeable topics and choices

A. NOTE: This starts with some choices that are fun.

B. You will then cover some examples of cultural differences.

C. Later, get into those things specific to your profession.

NOTE: You will need to ascertain whether or not you have any differently-abled people in the program who will not be able to quickly and comfortably move from one area of the room to the other. If you do have someone for whom this activity is physically difficult, you can modify it. Have them (or everyone) hold their arms out to the right or left rather than stand and move.

Do: Explain the activity to the participants.

Say: *In this activity you are going to have to get up and walk back and forth across the room. I will give the group a forced choice such as "coffee" or "tea." I will indicate which side of the room you should go to in order to demonstrate your preference. For example, if I say "Coffee, right,"* and you like coffee, go to your right (my left). Those who prefer tea, move to the opposite side of the room.

I will call out two things, and you have to decide which you prefer and go to where I point (e.g., to your right).

We will start with fun things and eventually get to things about your work and some cultural preferences.

Ask: Are there any questions?

Say: While you are deciding what you prefer, let me ask you to pay attention to several additional things:

- Patterns

- What other people prefer

- Lessons that might be learned from this activity about cultural diversity.

Say: OK, let's practice. When I say "Coffee, right; tea, left," go right for coffee and left for tea. (Because you are facing them and talking about their left and right, point to your left when you say right and to your right when you say left.)

Do: Start with the list on the left side of the sheet below. Go slowly enough to give people time not only to move to the sides of the room but also for laughing and talking.

Inevitably people will ask, "What if I like both?" My answer to that question is, "Which do you prefer? Pick one."

Sometimes they ask, "What do I do if I do not like either?" For example, vegetarians will not like either beef or pork. You can allow them to stand in the center of the room. If time permits you might ask them why they chose the middle before going on to the next choice for each set of choices. Once you let someone stand in the middle, others will join in.

When you get to the cultural preferences, name each one (see the sheet) and either tell them something about it or refer to a time later in the program when you will talk more about the Hofstede Dimensions and their orientations.

DEBRIEF THE ACTIVITY

Do: Allow them to remain standing.

Say: *When we started this activity, I asked you to think of lessons learned.*

Ask: *What did you learn about diversity from this activity?*

Expected Responses: *(Answers will vary)*

- There is a lot more to diversity than I thought.

- Everyone has very different preferences.

- I was surprised that my friends like so many different things than I do.

- You cannot identify a group of people and expect them to have the same preferences (it dispels the myth of "them" being alike).

- Every day we make lots of little choices about what we like and want; and everyone has different likes and dislikes.

Ask: What patterns did you see?

Expected Responses: (Answers will vary)

- What I noticed was that even people I thought ought to have similar preferences did not.

- I noticed that my friends has a lot of preferences different from mine.

- There were no discernible patterns.

Ask: What did it feel like to be in a group that was small or where you were alone?

Expected Responses: (Answers will vary)

- I am OK with that, but I can imagine that others might not be OK with that or it might make them uncomfortable.

- I chose to go with the group so as not to be singled out, alone, or in a small group.

- I was surprised that not so many people liked what I like.

Ask: What were some of the lessons you learned that you can take with you after this session?

Expected Responses: (Answers will vary)

- I need to pay more attention to what others are like and how they do things.

- Different is not wrong; it is just different.

- I might find out I like different things if I hang out with people who like different things.

FACILITATOR LIST OF PAIRED CHOICES

(NOTE: all pairs are optional. Feel free to add pairs that mean something to the attendees.)

GENERAL/FUN (Start here and do this side of the table first. Then go to Column 2)	CULTURAL
Coffee – tea	Read left to right – read right to left
Beef – pork	Miles – Kilometers
Salads – desserts	Fahrenheit – Celsius
Eat out – eat at home	An assignment with explicit instructions – one with general parameters (NEED FOR CERTAINTY – TOLERANCE FOR AMBIGUITY)
Potatoes – rice	
Cake – pie	Get the job done before going home for the day – going home on time to be with your family (ACHIEVEMENT – QUALITY OF LIFE ORIENTATION)
Bagels – sweet rolls	
Coke – Pepsi	Do it yourself – work in teams (INDIVIDUAL – GROUP)
7-up – Sprite	
Tap water – bottled	Clear organizational hierarchy – matrix organization (POWER DISTANCE)
Aerated water – still water	
Apartment – house	Live and/or work in your home country – Live and/or work outside your home country
Commute by train – commute by car	

Short hair – Long hair	Speak one language – speak more than one language
Professional dress – causal dress	**TRAINING**
Shore – mountains	Design – deliver
Read – go to the movies	Ask – tell
Vacation at home – vacation away	Manage others – manage self
Take a hike – ride a bike	Design content – design formatting of materials
Football – tennis	Soft skills training – Skills training
COMPUTERS	Simulations – role plays
Mac – PC	Presenting – facilitating
Working with computers – working with people	Managing – doing
Hardware – software	Travel – stay at home
	Line (business unit) – staff (HQ)
	Delivering classroom – on-line or blended
	Designing classroom – online or blended learning

Chapter 17
Culture Case Study Activity

Behaviors are driven by the underlying values that people hold. It is difficult to know what is impacting how people behave. A typical metaphor for culture is the iceberg because so much of what drives behaviors is "below the surface." What is unseen can have a hugely negative impact, which can come as a surprise.

The purpose of this activity is to allow team members to test whether they recognize cultural drivers of behaviors in real life situations.

This activity is best conducted after the team members have been introduced to the Hofstede dimensions, preferably after they have their cultural profile. For more information about the Culture in the Workplace Questionnaire™ (or CWQ), see Chapter 21.

At the end of the activity, participants will be able to:

- Identify cultural differences as presented in this case.

- Describe the impact of cultural misunderstandings.

- Identify the business risks when cultural misunderstandings occur.

- Make recommendations for how to avoid (and mitigate) the risks presented in this case.

Audience:

Employees working with global customers

Employees managed by people from other cultures

Managers who manage people from other cultures

Employees in the global supply chain

Call center employees who support global efforts or customers

PREPARATION CHECKLIST

Provide an assessment of cultural profiles so individuals can see their starting point. Introduce the aspects of each dimension. Then conduct this activity to see if they recognize cultural drivers when they see them in action.

- Make copies of the reading.

- Make a copy (for your use) of the Answer Key.

TIMING

	General Introductions	15 minutes
	Module Introduction	5 minutes
	Case Review and Discussion	15 minutes
	Group Report Outs	20 minutes
	Activity Debrief	5 minutes

DURING THE ACTIVITY

60 minutes

This activity provides a meeting scenario between a Dutch Leader of the Life Division of an insurance company and his "sponsor" in Yemen. There are several cultural differences highlighted. Learners are asked to identify them and come up with recommendations on how to avoid them in the future as well as how to mitigate the problems that have been caused by the cultural misunderstandings.

GENERAL INTRODUCTIONS

Do: If this is the first time this group is meeting together, facilitate introductions. Ask each learner any set of the questions provided to the right. Feel free to add other questions you think are relevant for these learners to know about each other.

Say: *Please provide your name, the languages you speak, and what you hope to get out of this case scenario. (Optional: the countries/cultures you have had experience working with.)*

MODULE INTRODUCTIONS

Do: Cover the objectives and tell the group what the purpose of this program is.

Say: *At the end of this session you should be able to:*

- *Identify cultural differences as presented in this case.*

- *Describe the impact of cultural misunderstandings.*

- *Identify the business risks when cultural misunderstandings occur.*

- *Make recommendations for how to avoid (and mitigate) the risks presented in this case.*

I am going to hand out a cultural case. I am going to ask each group to review the case, discuss what is happening in the scenario described, and work together to come up with answers to the questions provided.

Be prepared to present your case and recommendations to the larger group.

CASE REVIEW AND DISCUSSION

Do: Divide the learners into groups of three or more. Hand out the case.

Say: *You will have 15 minutes to work on this scenario.*

GROUP REPORT OUT

Do: Ask the groups if they have finished. Bring them all back to the larger group. Ask one group to answer the first question with three cultural differences.

Ask the rest of the groups what else they found.

Continue asking various groups their answers to the questions so that each group is heard. Allow other groups to ask questions or challenge the presenting groups' recommendations or responses.

Say: *The first question was "List some of the cultural differences described in this case."*

Ask: *Group xxx, what are three differences you found in this case?*

Expected Answers (not necessarily in this order):

- Attitudes about contracts

- Individual/group

- Business meetings

- Socializing

- Attitudes about time

- Security

- Wearing shoes in the house

- Eating and drinking

- Money/fees

- When to bring up business (what setting, with whom, at what kind of event)

- Relationship building/time spent

- Business consequences of not building relationships

- The relationship between past, present, and future.

DEBRIEF THE ACTIVITY

Do: Summarize

Say: *As you can see from this case, there were some serious business repercussions for the Dutch company due to their representative's lack of appreciation for cultural differences.*

Ask: *In what ways does your company take risks by not understanding cultural differences?*

Expected Answers:

- HR Hiring, selection, promotion, compensation.

- Marketing – product ingredients, product naming, product packaging.

- Sales – (see case below).

- Legal – contract formulation and requirements.

Say: *As leaders, we have fiduciary responsibility to avoid risks that will cost the company. Introducing the importance of cultural differences is a very inexpensive way to avoid risks.*

However, leaders also need to think through how to mitigate risks that may already have occurred due to cultural differences. For this, employees need a deeper understanding of what to do after cultural blunders have been made.

HANDOUT

DIRECTIONS:

- Read through the case provided below.

- Discuss the questions at the bottom of the case.

- Be prepared to present your findings to the larger group.

SCENARIO: [Note: This case applies to nearly all Middle Eastern countries.]

Mr. van den Hoeven is a native of the Netherlands. A graduate of the London School of Economics, he has grown through the ranks at this insurance company over the past ten years. He is generally seen among his peers as sharp and analytical, yet easy to get along with. He is a shrewd negotiator and has successfully handled complicated client situations. He has already served as Vice President in the UK and Country Manager in the Netherlands. Now he has been asked to lead this insurance company's Life Division in Yemen. This is a small but growing market, so it is seen as important to put an experienced professional in the position.

As in many countries in the Middle East, this insurance company's presence in Yemen exists under a "sponsorship." Selecting, arranging, and maintaining the sponsor relationship is important for doing business in Yemen, and a sponsor could either be a local person (tribal leader) or corporation. It is customary for the sponsor to collect a fee. This insurance company's sponsor in Yemen is Starboard Enterprises. Their main business is ship repair, but they also are involved in financial services and other industries. Much of this insurance company's success in Yemen has come from having access to Starboard's network of businesses. Starboard currently collects 0.5 percent from this insurance company's top line in Yemen. Specifically, this insurance company's relationship with Starboard is through Abdallah al-Hajri. Mr. al-Hajri is a cousin of the President and CEO of Starboard, Sheikh Mohammad al-Hajri.

Shortly after Mr. van den Hoeven's arrival in Yemen, Mr. al-Hajri invites van den Hoeven to a meeting at the family compound outside the city of Aden. The invitation does not specify a meeting time, and thinking this was just an opportunity to get acquainted, van den Hoeven goes to the meeting himself. His driver takes him to the compound gate. A security guard verifies that it is indeed Mr. van den Hoeven, after which he fires two brisk rounds with his rifle into the air. This sets in motion a flurry of activity in the house.

Mr. van den Hoeven is taken to an ornate sitting room. He walks into the room in a casual manner, but is quickly prompted to take off his shoes by the door. Three men are in the room. Mr. van den Hoeven walks right up to Abdallah al-Hajri, not realizing that the person to his left is Sheikh Mohammad al-Hajri. Mr. van den Hoeven is offered assorted fruits, tea and juice. Green leaves are in tea cup sized bowls. The hosts all put the leaves in their mouths and insist their guest try some, but he declines.

The conversation goes well and the hosts ask many questions about Mr. van den Hoeven's world travels. After about 30 minutes, the following conversation takes place:

al-Hajri: Respectfully, sir, we have to increase our sponsorship fee.

van den Hoeven: [long pause as this comes as a surprise] Also with respect, we have a ten-year agreement with a fixed term that was signed just two years ago.

al-Hajri: Oh yes, Mr. van den Hoeven. You have been in our region for very little time. Would you like me to arrange for you to visit and understand our country better? Perhaps I could arrange a weekend of informal activity. We should get to know you. As for this contract matter, I understand that this will take some time for you to consider. Unfortunately, circumstances have changed. No one can predict what the future will hold. Due to these changes, we have to increase the sponsorship fee to three percent.

van den Hoeven: I have read our agreement, and it does not allow fee changes due to changes in circumstances. I can't accept this request. I am sure that as a responsible business man you can accept that your company has signed a legally binding agreement with our company. I believe the simplest course of action would be to have our respective legal departments have a look at the agreement. We can then have a factual discussion on what is possible—if anything—to change in the current contract.

al-Hajri: But circumstances have changed, so I must insist. You are referring to the legal departments. I was lead to believe that you were the man in charge in your organization. This is a matter of great importance that we must discuss.

van den Hoeven: I also must insist. I do not know the exact contract terms off hand and I repeat, I do not have the agreement with me. There is little point in our discussing further this topic without a factual basis. I am accustomed to doing business in a professional manner. Furthermore, I would like to remind you that my company will insist that your company act in a legally responsible manner in relation to this agreement which you signed. On return to the office, I will put this matter in the hands of our legal staff. They will get back to you in a timely fashion. If you excuse me, it has been a pleasure to meet with you. I have to get back to the office now. I have a lot of work to do (looking at his watch).

Within a week, sales agents are reporting an increase in dropped policies. HR is reporting difficulty recruiting new sales agents. After two weeks, the Yemeni Tax Department orders a full audit on this insurance company in Yemen. They find irregularities and fine this insurance company. Starboard says it is considering withdrawing sponsorship.

CASE STUDY QUESTIONS:

1. Mr. van den Hoven, who is Dutch, ranks high on Individual Orientation. Members of Arab cultures are more likely to tend towards Collectivism/Group Orientation. Assumptions about contracts, laws, and rules tend to be different in Arab and Dutch cultures as well. List some of the cultural differences described in this case.

2. Perceptions about time are very different in Arab cultures versus Dutch and many other Western cultures. How did this case illustrate that difference?

3. Preferences regarding personal relationships at work are also different between these cultures. How did that difference impact this situation?

4. What recommendations might you make to:

    *   Prepare for a potential cross-cultural situation like the one described here?

    *   Make better decisions in these kinds of situations (where cultural differences are impacting effective working interactions)?

    *   Help Messers Mr. van den Hoeven and al-Hajri repair any miscommunication after this interaction?

Please explain your suggestions.

Handout Answer Key

1. Western cultures tend to view law books and legal rulings as the absolute truth. In many non-western cultures, including Arab cultures, rules exist in context and the context may change. Fate and beliefs about God also influence how Arab cultures deal with rules and regulations. Often, rules are not written.

2. Arab cultures may take longer to accept change than the Dutch culture. In this case the long-term quality of the relationship between the parties should have been the priority for all involved to get a positive outcome.

3. In many Western cultures, there are either sharp lines between personal friendships and professional relationships, or professional relationships are casual. These lines are more blurred in Arab cultures, and it is common to see personal relationships at work. These personal relationships can create decision-making at work that Westerners might consider not objective or even nepotistic (not to say that favoritism can't occur in any culture).

4. Ask a local what the meeting is really about before going. You may, if appropriate to the host, bring a local to the meeting. Learn local customs and traditions. Be aware of who holds positions of authority and interact with them appropriately. Do not react strongly to situations and be aware of your emotions. Making a decision on the spot may not be wise. Interpret events afterwards with a local to determine their meaning.

yes

how this
get done +
how get laws
around laws
+ rules (of personal connection)

Success on teams is directly related to the level of trust and relationships team members have and exhibit. It is much more difficult to build trust after an incident that has created a trust gap. Focusing on how team members start out (trusting or needing to build trust) is an important activity for teams to undertake early on.

This activity helps team members better understand what other members of their teams believe to be important to building and maintaining a level of trust. It also helps team leaders understand what kind of team protocols will help build trust and relationships.

Team leaders can bring the trust issue into the open by starting project team interactions with the following activity, which begins the discussion about who trusts whom and what is it that breaks trust for anyone on the team. The team leader can then use this information to begin the establishment of team protocols for how the team members will work together (their human process interactions).

Below you can find an activity that will help teams begin to set working protocols.

At the end of the activity, participants will be able to:

- List those specific behaviors others on this team see as building trusting work/team relationships.

- List those specific behaviors others on this team see as breaking trust.

- Discuss communication and meeting protocols that will help all team members feel trusted.

Audience: Teams in virtual meetings

PREPARATION CHECKLIST

Presentation equipment that all virtual team members can access (such as GoToMeeting or Adobe Connect).

TIMING

Activity Instructions	2 minutes
Activity	Up to 45 minutes
Debrief	15 minutes

DURING THE ACTIVITY

NOTE: Use the time in one of your team meetings to ask each of your team members to explain their approach to trust by responding to a set of questions.

Say: *Since trust is so important to building successful teams, we are going to discuss how we come to trust other team members. I will be asking you each to answer some questions about how you come to trust others and what bars or breaks trust on teams. I want you to start thinking about these questions.*

I am going to ask each of you to respond to these questions so others in the group know more about how to interact with you effectively. First I will ask each of you to share whether you implicitly trust or whether others need to show they are trustworthy. Then I will go around again and ask each of you questions so I can start collecting information and your opinions on what behaviors on teams break trust or create barriers to trust.

When we are finished with that, I will ask you to work together in small groups to make recommendation for protocols or rules we can consider that will help us avoid many of the problems that typically occur on teams.

Ask each person by name: *Are you someone who implicitly trusts others? Do they have to do something to betray or lose your trust? Or are you someone who is more skeptical at first so that others have to win your trust?*

Expected answers: They will either answer that they trust first or that someone needs to earn their trust.

Do: Ask each person by name whether they implicitly trust others. If they start to talk about why they feel this is so, ask them to hold their thoughts for the next questions which will relate to what builds or breaks trust on teams.

Do: After each person has had a chance to answer, turn on the PowerPoint with a column on the right side. (See sample above in "Preparation.")

Say: *Now that we know a little about our trusting styles, let's find out more about behaviors that are barriers to trust. I am going to ask each of you, "What team behaviors break trust?" Or "What behaviors are the barriers to trust?"*

Ask: *What behaviors might cause you not to trust or might cause you to lose trust in your team mates?*

Do: Type in their answers on the PowerPoint slide. Make sure you number their answers for easier reference later. Create additional slides as necessary.

Expected Answers: These can range from simple things such as,
- "Not responding when I say hi in the morning," to,
- "Not responding when I send an email or leave a voice mail message."

Do: Write down their answers on the first PowerPoint and number the issues.

Call on each person in turn and let them answer the questions. Record all their answers in a numbered list. When everyone has had a turn, ask if there are any more topics that should be included on the slide.

Do: Add any additional comments and number them. When they are satisfied that all their team issues are on the slide...

Say: *With this list of potential issues on teams, we are going to have to find ways to mitigate or avoid these behaviors.*

Do: Put them into small groups (even virtually; you can use natural culture groups or location groups). Either end the call and reestablish contact in 20 minutes, or use a technology that allows groups to go into virtual break-out rooms. Adobe Connect has this feature. If you do not have this capability, you can either leave the line open or call back in 20 minutes. Assign them the task to come up with specific team behaviors and communication protocols that will mitigate or avoid some of the issues listed on the slides. Give them 20 minutes to work together to come up with communication and behavior protocols. Ask each group to report out.

Say: *I am going to ask each group to report out their suggestions. When you offer a suggestion, make sure you tell me the number of the issue on this list (refer to the slide[s]) that your suggestion mitigates.*

Do: Allow them to discuss ideas suggested. You might need to probe for embellishment of the suggestion, or you might want to get input from other team members about the suggestion.

Capture each idea on the PowerPoint. Number it with the issue number.

You Could Ask (for example): *Are there ways to improve this suggestion? What might you suggest we do in addition to this idea?*

DEBRIEF THE ACTIVITY

Do: Make sure each item on the list has a suggestion and a check mark. If not, question them about what to do to avoid that item.

(Participative Approach) Hold a discussion about which of the ideas the team is willing to adopt as team rules for how they will interact with each other.

(Hierarchical Approach) Determine which suggestions should become team rules and let them know your decision on the spot.

Make sure the "rules" include the following topics (the rules may not be limited to these topics):

- Voice mail messaging
- How to structure emails including how to use the subject line and who to include or copy
- How to ask for needed information
- How to give information (how much context)
- Which technologies are preferred by each team member
- Distribution list creation
- Minutes/notes/action items recording
- Commitments made to get things accomplished by a specific time
- What to do if commitments cannot be met
- How (and when) to notify others about missing deadlines.

Ask: What did you learn from this activity?

Expected Answers: These will vary but will likely be focused on learning about each other's styles and learning how to behave in ways that make working together more effective.

Especially for those with members who have Group and/or Quality of Life Orientations, knowing something about other team members improves collaboration and relationship building. When teams are virtual, this is especially important.

The purpose of this activity is to get the team to share about themselves and to get them talking about their expectations of other team members and the team leader.

This is either an individual activity (Individual Orientation) or a group activity (using small groups for those with Group Orientation). It requires some conversation about expectations of team members and often helps start the conversation about team protocols that may need to be set. This discussion helps the team leader understand what the team members expect. It is best conducted early in the team's work.

At the end of the activity, participants will be able to:

- Describe the needs and expectations of other team members.

- List team protocols they have developed to meet team members expectations.

- Describe expectations that were unrealistic and will not be met.

Audience:

- Team members with either Individual or Group Orientation.

- Participative Orientation team members.

Note that the in-person instructions work best for team members with Individual/Achievement Orientations. Collectivist cultures (Group Orientation) are not as adept at sharing individual feelings and ideas. They are more comfortable discussing what the group thinks. So when conducting this activity in-person with Group-oriented team members, use small groups to discuss the information and let the smaller groups provide aggregate answers.

If you are working with those from Asian or Latin countries or are having a virtual meeting, you might use Survey Monkey to ask the questions, aggregate their answers and share the aggregate answers with the group on PowerPoint (GoToMeeting, GoToWebinar, Adobe Connect, or other applications).

This activity offers options for use with a co-located team (or for use at an in-person team meeting where all members are present) or a virtual meeting.

Preparation Checklist

For in-person meetings, you will need flip charts and pens.

For virtual meetings, you will need presentation equipment.

For a virtual meeting, create an on-line survey (such as SurveyMonkey) and send out a link with instructions on when they are to have completed their responses.

A WEEK PRIOR TO THE SESSION (In-Person Meeting)

Make copies of the question sheet.

A WEEK PRIOR TO THE SESSION (Virtual Meeting)

- Aggregate the data and look for themes.

- Prepare the results on PowerPoint or some other presentation application.

- Send out the questions and request the meeting attendees fill it out and be prepared to share their answers with the entire group.

Timing

	Activity set up	5 minutes
	Virtual Meeting	
	Activity/Presentation	5 – 10 minutes
	Activity Sharing and Discussion	20 minutes
	In-Person Meeting	
	Activity/Answering the questions	20 minutes
	Activity/Sharing and Discussion	20 minutes
	Debrief	15 minutes

BEFORE THE ACTIVITY, IF VIRTUAL

Do: Explain why you asked them to respond to the survey and what is going to happen with the results.

Say: *The purpose of this activity is to help others, including the team leader, better understand your expectations as a member of this team. As a result of this activity, we will have a better understanding about what expectations are unreal or that we cannot meet them. We will also have a better understanding of what our team members need from each other. As a team leader, I will have a better understanding of what team members need from me.*

DURING THE ACTIVITY, IF VIRTUAL

Say: *I have aggregated the results from the responses to the survey and will present them to you. Then I will ask each of you to tell us your responses to the questions I sent out earlier for you to think about.*

Do: Present the aggregate answers and either ask each person to share their answers if you used list of questions on page 199, or share all the answers if you chose to put all the questions on the on-line survey.

Answers will vary to these questions. (See the questions in the Handout/Survey section.)

DEBRIEF THE ACTIVITY

Do: Use their answers to manage the expectations of the group. For example, if they expect to learn how to be an effective team leader so they can lead teams in the future, you might point out that while they can use your behavior as a model, there will not be time or any other focus on learning how to be team leader. Also, as a team leader you will not be in any position to recommend who would learn how to be an effective team leader. However, you would appreciate if team members gave you feedback when you did something that they felt was particularly effective (or not). This is a Participative approach.

Use their answers to offer protocols (rules) that the team adheres to in order to make their work together more efficient. As a Hierarchical leader, you can tell them what protocols you will institute. For a more Participative approach, ask for their input and collaborate on the decisions about team rules.

NOTE: In virtual meetings a slightly more Hierarchical approach works best due to the problems with getting everyone's opinion and people talking over each other.

DURING THE ACTIVITY, IF IN PERSON

Do: Give them time to complete the questions before starting the discussion.

Say: *The purpose of this activity is to help others, including the team leader, better understand your expectations as a member of this team. As a result of this activity, we will have a better understanding about what expectations are unrealistic or that we cannot meet. We also will have a better understanding of what our team members need from each other. As a team leader, I will have a better understanding of what team members need from me.*

Say: *I am going to give you time to answer these questions, and then we will share the answers. There are no correct or incorrect answers. Please tell us what you want and need in order to make the team leader, the team, and team meetings effective. You can work together in small groups or you can work alone.*

I will give you 20 minutes and then check back with you to see if you need more time.

MY CONNECTION TO THE TEAM: HANDOUT OR ELECTRONIC SURVEY QUESTIONS

(Option 1) DIRECTIONS FOR CO-LOCATED RESPONDENTS:

Using the table below, fill in your answers and be prepared to discuss them with the larger group. You will have 20 minutes to think about and write down your answers.

(Option 2) DIRECTIONS FOR SURVEY RESPONDENTS:

Using the table below, fill in your answers to these questions. I will aggregate the answers and share them at the meeting on [insert date here]. Please complete your responses before close of business on [insert date here].

1. I am... (Describe yourself in several short words of phrases. Be prepared to elaborate.)

2. I bring these capabilities and competencies to the team... (List the most important ones for the team members and team leader to know about you.)

3. These things interest me about being a member of this team...

4. In general, these things have annoyed me about the behaviors of team members when I have been on other teams...

5. Team members can expect the following from me... (What is your commitment to the team?)

6. What I expect from my team members includes...

7. What I expect from the team leader includes...

8. While a member of this team, I hope to learn...

9. To be an effective member of this team, it would help me to know this about my team members...

10. To be an effective member of this team, it would help me to know this about the team leader...

One of the major complaints on teams is that people do not communicate enough, do not share the more important things, do not respond quickly enough, or are not available when others need them. Teams who do not attend early to their potential communication problems often face eroding trust and loss of efficiencies. This activity is designed to help teams focus on what kinds of barriers they will face in their remote communications with other team members.

This activity gets virtual team members to focus on issues that may occur with internal communications. It also helps focus the team on issues that may occur with external communications between business teams working on related projects or working toward the same goals.

At the end of the activity, participants will be able to:

- Pay attention to cultural issues and how these issues might impact trust and team work.

- Describe agreed upon communications protocols within the team and with others outside the team.

Audience:

All remote team members.

PREPARATION CHECKLIST

Send out the meeting agenda and explain the purpose of the activity.

Include a copy of the questions (see below) and ask them to bring the question sheet to the meeting. Explain that they will be given time to respond to the questions during the meeting and that they will be expected to fill in their respective answers and submit them to be shared.

TIMING

	Activity Instructions	2 minutes
	Activity	5 minutes
	Debrief	5 minutes

DURING THE ACTIVITY

Say: *The challenge for distant teams is to find the best ways to communicate and to carry out the work of the team. Communication is required in many different areas:*

1.   *Within the team—communication between team members is especially critical on distant and global teams.*

2.   *Between teams that are working on related projects.*

3.   *Between the team, outside individuals, and groups that either provide resources to support the work of the team, help to implement the work of the team, or are the team's clients.*

As you think through how we are going to work together, consider this question:

What factors influence whether communications on global teams are effective or not?

Here are some topics of concern regarding communication for global teams that we need to consider.

- *How information should be shared (both before and after meetings), how often and in what mode (paper, internet, email).*

- *Responsiveness to others on the team (how quickly one responds and in what mode).*

- *Information sharing (what, with whom and how often), what is regular and what is special.*

- *Communication (I only find out about things if I happen to contact someone on your site, why can't I be regularly informed of changes or updated?)*

Say: *In order to be effective in communicating with each other, we first need to understand the best way to get the quickest response from each other. So I need each of you to fill out the questionnaire I sent out prior to the meeting. Please submit it to me (or my assistant) by [insert date here] and we will distribute the results to everyone.*

Ask: *Do you have any questions about what I am requesting?*

Do: If so, answer their questions.

Refer to the questionnaire below. Ask them to spend five minutes answering all the questions and to email that back to you. Stay available to answer any questions.

Do: After five minutes draw or show this graphic.

Use of Technology

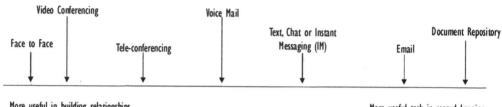

Say: *As we begin to work together, please recognize that we will need to build relationships and trust among team members. Some methods of technology are better for building relationships and others are better for information sharing (more task-focused). Please think about this graphic as you are thinking about working with your colleagues who are remote from your location.*

I want you to pick up the telephone or schedule a video conference if you have not yet worked extensively with particular colleagues. You can do so outside of team meetings.

The purpose of this is to find ways to get to know each other better. While some of us prefer just to get to work, others may need to see our faces and get to know a little about us before they can trust us.

HANDOUT/ON-LINE QUESTIONNAIRE

DIRECTIONS:

Fill in your answers to the following questions. This will help us understand how to contact each other and which technologies each of us prefer. You will be given time in the meeting on [insert meeting date/times]. After the meeting, please submit this to me [my assistant] via email at my email address [or my assistant's] [insert email address here].

1.   Name: _____

2.   I preferred to be called: _____

3.   My location: _____

[This can be building number, city, mail stop, etc. Specify what you want them to include; choose what is most useful to your team.]

4.   Technology I have access to for team meetings: _____ [or you can give them a check list and ask them to choose what they have access to]

5.   Please contact me first by (which mode of technology): _____

6.   You can reach me at (phone number, email address, Skype address or other way team members can reach you at your preferred technology): _____

7.   My second preference is (which mode of technology): _____

8.   If my first preference does not get a response, you can try to reach me at (phone number, email address, Skype address or other way team members can reach you at your preferred technology): _____

[NOTE: You can also collect any other useful information such as office hours, internal bridge numbers or extensions, home email addresses, cell numbers, etc.]

DEBRIEF THE ACTIVITY

OPTIONAL DEBRIEF SUGGESTIONS: To stimulate thinking with a more participative group you can raise issues for discussion such as those below. Topics of concern for global teams, in addition to normal team issues, may include:

- Timing of the meetings (Someone is working after or before hours to accommodate the others.)

- Mode of the meetings (Someone has to travel or make videoconferencing arrangements or hotel accommodations.)

- Budget issues (Why do I always have to pay for travel, video conferencing services, or secretarial support?)

- Who should be included in the meetings or appraised?

- How information should be shared (both before and after meetings), how often, and in what mode (paper, internet, email).

- Responsiveness to others on the team (how quickly one responds and in what mode).

- Information sharing (what, with whom. and how often). What is regular and what is special?

- The amount of support services (e.g., secretarial) given to the team.

- Cross-cultural misunderstandings (You dismiss what I say, you don't respect my opinion, the leader is not enough of this or too much of that, when I call you your secretary returns my call, etc.)

- Access to leadership (The team leader is more accessible to you because you are located together.)

- Decision making (You make decisions when I am not there and just tell me what you have decided. You do not tell me when you change priorities until several weeks after the decision, and I have been wasting time working on the old priorities.)

- Communication (I only find out about things if I happen to contact someone on your site; why can't I be regularly informed of changes or updated?)

You might ask some provocative questions. Here are some examples of what might be raised for discussion:

- Why do the "a's" (e.g., Europeans) have more secretarial support than the "b's" (e.g., Americans)?

- You don't appreciate that you have help getting travel arrangements, planning and coordinating meetings or conferences, taking messages, replying, sending materials back and forth, etc. I have to do all my own without support (or I have to share my support staff with five other people).

- Why do the "x" (e.g., West coast scientists) always have to be the ones to travel for business meetings?

- Why are the meetings always done in "q" (e.g., Japanese)?

- Why does it take so long for you to answer my voicemail (or email)?

- Why do you always CC your boss on replies to my email when this is just between us?

- When I email you, why do you insist on answering me on voicemail?

- Why isn't there a marketing (or finance, IT, or regulatory) representative on the product discovery team?

- Why do I always have to be the one who meets after hours (or before) because of the time differences between our locations?

- Can we get an agenda at least one day prior to the meetings so those of us who speak English as a second language can prepare in advance?

- Can we invite someone from the "f" team to our meetings so they know what is going on?

- Can we send someone from our meetings to the "f" team?

- Why do I always have to pay for travel, videoconferencing, or support services out of my budget? You are part of corporate, and my budget items come off the bottom line. Yours don't.

who get this?

Chapter 21
Culture in the Workplace Questionnaire™ (CWQ)

Culture, which Dr. Hofstede refers to as "software of the mind/mental programming," is a critical variable that guides peoples' actions and reactions. Understanding one's own culture and the impact of culture on the actions of others is essential for effective global business interactions. ITAP's The Culture in the Workplace Questionnaire™ (CWQ) provides insights about the respondent's cultural preferences as well as the cultural preferences of others. It provides a framework for understanding diverse approaches to workplace interactions such as problem solving, working in teams, and managing projects.

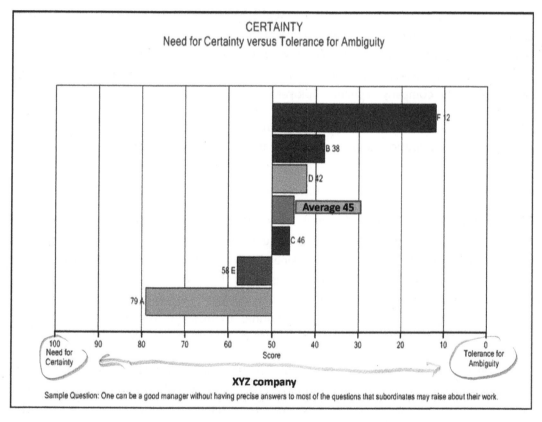

CERTAINTY
Need for Certainty versus Tolerance for Ambiguity

XYZ company

Sample Question: One can be a good manager without having precise answers to most of the questions that subordinates may raise about their work.

The Culture in the Workplace Questionnaire™ is derived from the work of Dr. Geert Hofstede. This instrument provides an individual profile compared against country averages. It is available in English, German, French, European Spanish, Latin American Spanish, Chinese, Korean and Arabic. A questions-only version (with questions/answer scale but not the reports) is available in Danish and Japanese.

BUSINESS CASE FOR CULTURAL UNDERSTANDING: RISK MITIGATION

The CWQ helps improve productivity, reduces the cost of rework, improves client services, avoids the unintended consequences of demotivating employees who are culturally diverse, and avoids unintentional discrimination.

USES FOR THE CWQ WITH INDIVIDUALS

The CWQ has been used to help create a global mindset for large international companies when administered to the new employees and debriefed in the new employee onboarding process or orientation. The CWQ helps establish a common, non-threatening language around differences, and it introduces the expectation that, as a global organization, the company expects employees to respect cultural differences.

The CWQ also has been used with many employee development scenarios in global or multi-cultural organizations and for executive and/or relocation coaching.

USES FOR THE CWQ WITH GLOBAL WORKFORCE DEVELOPMENT

Many cross-cultural training programs offer the "Do's and Don'ts" of international business, often mixing information about etiquette with advice on what types of business gifts to give and how to best form business relationships in specific countries. These programs are most useful for employees with little or no international business experience. At the end of these programs, participants know that there are cultural differences and know how they should handle themselves in situations or cultures covered in these programs.

The CWQ provides information instead on foundational cultural differences based on the Hofstede dimensions. These can be applied regardless of with whom one works (even colleagues from the same culture who may have different cultural orientations). This approach helps learners look for underlying cultural values based on behaviors they can observe. It also focuses on how they might be more effective when interacting in a wide variety of scenarios with those who do things differently.

The CWQ has been embedded in training programs where it is important for employees and managers to understand how culture impacts communication, delegation, motivation, and other tasks in performance management, negotiations, conflict resolution, project management, customer service, product naming, and in the design of collateral materials. It often is used in country debriefs for groups.

At a high level, CWQ information and analytics are brought to bear on specific strategic issues for analysis and improvement. These have included:

1.   Specific business problems or opportunities (e.g., sales or marketing, mergers or acquisitions).

2.   Decision-making at upper levels (e.g., where to locate a new plant in a region).

3.   Functional transformations (e.g., transforming Finance or HR to be more strategic and global).

4.   Change management (e.g., analyzing or conducting a gap analysis on internal values, measured by the CWQ, to identify barriers to change).

At the end of these interventions, employees are able to apply the analytic tools and specific country, regional, and culture-based information to other business problems and practices.

USES FOR THE CWQ WITH GLOBAL VIRTUAL TEAMS

Not only does the CWQ provide individual cultural profiles, it also can display comparison bar charts and quadrant charts (comparing any two-dimensional results) for the use of teams and/or groups. It has been used in training plus in the comparisons of teams and of team members and to help the teams establish protocols for working together to make them more productive and efficient. For example, this chart displays the country scores for Individualism and Power Distance which together relate to the similarities or differences in the general country work styles and approaches to decision making.

Culture impacts team members' expectations of their team leader and their perspectives on what they believe makes an effective team member. When discussing barriers to effective interactions, the CWQ results help individuals and teams see how cultural values may be at play. This helps them open up to a variety of ways of operating effectively by, for example, using telephone and voice mail for those who are more relationship oriented (or who just prefer the personal touch) and email for those who are more task oriented.

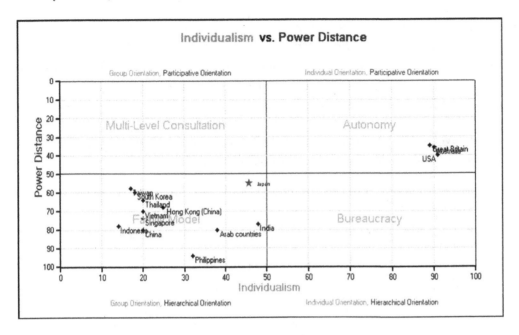

USES FOR THE CWQ WITH ORGANIZATIONS

<u>**Change Management/Transformation Analysis**</u>: By measuring the cultures of the division vs. HQ or cutting the data by function, age, gender, length of service, or other demographics collected, the client can design a change approach by organizational sub-culture.

Differences: Power Distance & Certainty

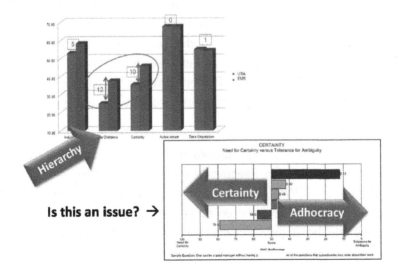

Mergers/Acquisitions: In merger and acquisition situations, the CWQ can provide information on the values of various groups, and clients can use the data to assess where to expect barriers to change. This information allows companies to understand where to apply more attention. For example, for groups with need for certainty, communicate more often or with more depth.

Organizational or Marketing Research: The CWQ has been used in various research scenarios including:

- Assessing the cultural differences by country in gifting and recognition practices.

- Analyzing customer reactions by country to call center agents in the health advice and on-line servicing of medical devices.

- Measuring the impact of culture on attitudes towards risk and safety for a large oil platform construction company.

- Conducting culture audits on training materials to see if they match the cultural values of the learners and trainers in outsourcing scenarios and realigning the learning content and instructor materials to be culturally appropriate.

- Measuring the Asian/American differences in offshore back office processing.

FEATURES AND BENEFITS OF THE CULTURE IN THE WORKPLACE QUESTIONNAIRE™ (CWQ)

CWQ FEATURES	CWQ BENEFITS
The questionnaire is completely web-enabled.	This makes it easy to administer and complete. The facilitator can choose to have individual users' questionnaire results display immediately or deliver the results at the learning session.
The questionnaire is available on a secure website, and results can be distributed electronically through Acrobat pdf files.	Clients can fill out the questionnaire from anywhere in the world. Consultants can print out results from anywhere in the world. (Reduces time and mailing costs.)
The questionnaire was developed by Dr. Geert Hofstede and includes questions designed by Dr. André Laurent.	The research basis and association with some of the world's leading experts in the intercultural field increases the validity of the tool. Research that creates the country results is published and widely available in Hofstede's *Culture's Consequences*.
The questionnaire produces a respondent's cultural profile on five dimensions: Individualism, Power Distance, Certainty, Achievement, and Time Orientation.	Because there are only five dimensions, the information is easy to learn, remember, and apply in a business setting.

Report this in my comments

CWQ FEATURES	CWQ BENEFITS
Respondents can be given a choice of countries for comparison (from a 60+ country database of national averages) or provided with a pre-specified group of countries for comparison.	Allows the user's report to be customized to display countries of particular interest.
The graphs contained in the user's report are available in two versions: the original vertical version or the new horizontal version.	The facilitator can decide which version to use for each project or program.
The user's report contains a results summary that identifies the respondent's cultural preferences and, for each dimension, provides an individualized results explanation as well as an individualized expert analysis of the user's scores and their scores compared to country data.	Helps the respondent understand the information about the dimension and internalize it to a specific business setting. Makes it easy for respondents to identify the impact of their cultural preferences on others and therefore helps improve communications and productivity.
The questionnaire is a learner-focused instrument.	A facilitator can help participants focus the questionnaire results on the participants' workplace. Use of the questionnaire can help minimize culture-based misunderstandings, improve cross-cultural relationships, and develop global mindsets in employees.
The respondent learns how an awareness of workplace preferences can be useful in a variety of business situations, both at home and abroad.	The learning has broad applicability. Once the respondent is familiar with the dimensions and their associated workplace behaviors, appropriate adjustments can be made when interacting with people from any culture.
The system can be set up to automatically generate team or group bar charts and country bar charts for each dimension.	The facilitator can use these additional materials to facilitate learning about team dynamics and how the team's or group's results compare to different country averages.
Each CW project has a designated facilitator.	Facilitators can manage their own programs. They have online access to information about the questionnaire completion status for users in their programs, can send reminder emails, and can view and print individual user and group reports.
Customized demographics can be chosen by clients.	Data can be analyzed according to specific client needs. For example, clients may wish to know the cultural differences between different operational locations in different countries to improve training or to consider different employee reward systems.

Chapter 22
Global Team Process Questionnaire™ (GTPQ)

Measuring human process interactions on teams helps leaders, especially those on virtual or cross-cultural teams, keep current with how well the team interactions are progressing (or regressing). Periodic measurement not only provides information about the current state but over time, but progress can be measured and shared with the team members as they become high performing.

THE TEAM PROCESS QUESTIONNAIRE SYSTEM

The Team Process Questionnaire System (TPQS) supports the development of teams and team leaders and provides business leaders with critical information on the effectiveness of their initiatives across teams and team members. Using the TPQ System results in improvements both on individual teams and in the management of teams.

There are three versions of the TPQS process: 1) The Global Team Process Questionnaire™ (GTPQ), 2) the Organizational Team Process Questionnaire™ (OTPQ), and 3) the Action Learning Team Process Questionnaire™ (ALTPQ). The ALTPS is useful on Action Learning teams that may have been assigned a learning coach or for those that are self-directed teams. These instruments provide periodic team wellness checks, and filling out the online instrument is time efficient because takes about 20 to 30 minutes per person per iteration.

The information and analysis from the results can improve:

1. Team Leader Coaching (GTPQ/OTPQ): Provides data for consultants coaching team leaders.

2. Team Interventions: The TPQ system provides facilitators with specific data for interventions. The intervention becomes team specific, not method specific.

3. Management Oversight: Provides the company or division leaders with metrics for determining process and performance throughout a set of teams. The TPQ system also provides leadership with critical information about the influence of policy changes on teams and team members.

HOW DO THE TEAM PROCESS QUESTIONNAIRES SUPPORT TEAMS?

The Global Team Process Questionnaire™ (GTPQ) measures human processes on global teams. It provides a baseline for the global team's current state of human process interactions. Against that baseline, companies can measure change, identify areas for improvement, compare their results to industry averages, and measure the successes needed to figure out the actual return on investment.

The Organizational Team Process Questionnaire™ (OTPQ) has characteristics quite similar to the GTPQ, but it is designed for teams with membership from a single country.

Key uses in consulting interventions:

- To determine the level of process effectiveness on teams.

- To measure the level of process effectiveness on such teams over time.

- To compare process effectiveness to productivity.

- To diagnose the type of training intervention that will be most effective in improving a team's process effectiveness.

- To compare the process effectiveness of different teams working on the same or similar projects.

- To compare process effectiveness on specific teams with norms in the same industry.

IMPROVING COMPETITIVE ADVANTAGE

Use the TPQ system to:

- Improve productivity and results
  - By helping teams and team leaders identify appropriate areas for improvement.
  - By utilizing successful team leaders and their teams on the most critical projects.

- Affirm team members
  - By improving morale, reducing turnover, or both.
  - By investing in and developing team members.

- Develop leadership and manage succession – By identifying strong or weak team leaders and using that data to:
  - Provide development support to new, less-experienced or faltering team leaders.
  - Set up a leadership mentoring system.

- Be fiscally responsible – By reducing the costs usually associated with training and development through focusing on assessed needs.

- Encourage innovation and growth – By comparing global team data against industry norms and establishing baselines, continuous improvement can be measured.

ANALYZING TEAM ISSUES

The TPQ can provide focused information on:

- Team strengths and weaknesses.

- Team alignment or misalignment.

- Unexpected sub-team formation.

- Problems developing as a result of ineffectively acculturating new team members.

- Effect of team leadership.

- Impact of organizational changes or initiatives.

USING THE TPQ SYSTEM

The TPQ should be administered *at the right time, which is NOT at inception*. This tool is NOT a substitute for team chartering.

The TPQ should be administered after the team has had a chance to crystallize, to cohere from a group to a team. This time will depend to some extent on the frequency, length, and intensity of team meetings, but generally an intensive couple of days of team meetings are sufficient to have a team coalesce around goals, objectives, roles and responsibilities, and other critical team issues.

Teams that have shorter life spans—say, of three months—are often intensive project teams. For example, teams in the software industry or "mission critical" change projects. These teams typically gel quickly; interventions should also be provided quickly to help the team in its early stages.

where set?

THREE TYPES OF TPQ QUESTIONS

The TPQ Questionnaires include both quantitative and qualitative questions. The total number of questions is usually kept to about 35 to 45, which allows most respondents to answer the questionnaire in about 20 to 30 minutes. It's important to understand one of the unique features of the TPQ Questionnaires: the three types of questions.

- **Core Questions:** Core questions are normally **not** modified unless the question for some reason could not be answered by the team. There are qualitative and quantitative core questions, from which a database of responses has been collected.

- **Optional Questions:** These are often questions which started out as Custom Questions but are now on their way to becoming Core Questions; they may be selected by team leaders or consultants to add to the core questions. Results to these questions are not compared against the database.

- **Custom Questions:** Custom questions developed are usually team-specific and give the team the opportunity to tailor the quantitative or qualitative questions to meet the team's special requirements.

BASELINE

The first TPQ administration produces the baseline against which all subsequent administrations of the tool can be compared. The TPQ requires a second iteration, usually more. The second administration is accomplished after a suitable interval, in teams with longevities of a year or more—every three months, typically. However, every team is different, and the team and it's leader may want a unique schedule.

SUMMATIVE EVALUATION/LESSONS LEARNED

It can be useful to have the TPQ administered as the curtain falls on a team. At that point, team members have had an opportunity to process what has occurred across the full life cycle of the team and to reflect on it. This information, typically lost, can be as valuable to future teams as exit interviews are to future employees.

FEATURES AND BENEFITS OF THE TEAM PROCESS QUESTIONNAIRE™ SYSTEM

TPQ FEATURES	TPQ BENEFITS
The questionnaire is short (approximately 30 to 40 questions).	This makes it easy to administer and complete. The average time for a participant to fill out his/her answers is 20 to 30 minutes per quarter.
The core questions are used to collect industry norms. ITAP has many years of existing data on industry norms.	Industry norms can be used as targets to improve the company's competitive advantage.
The questionnaire is fully web-enabled. Results can be viewed online or distributed through Acrobat PDF files.	Team members can answer the questionnaire at any time and from anywhere in the world. Electronic collection of data and distribution of results reduces paper usage and time from data collection to reporting results.
The questionnaire design is flexible. Custom questions can be added to the core questions. Company, department, function, or specific team data (e.g., performance metrics) can be collected.	Provides data useful to make decisions at the company, department, functional, team, and individual levels.
There are both quantitative (Likert-scale) and qualitative questions. In the case of each quantitative question, the respondent is encouraged to provide accompanying comments.	Provides not only a numerical index to areas that are strong or weak, but an indication of the causal factors involved via comments of respondents.
The OTPQ allows same-company reviews of teams working on similar goals.	Provides leaders with a method of cross-team comparison, monitoring, and support.
Results are shared with the team leader and the leader is coached to support needed changes in the team.	This helps develop team leaders without taking them off the job. It provides them with behind the scenes support for the development of their team.
Results are shared with the team members and include: team averages	Providing the team these data points and discussing differences at regular team

TPQ FEATURES	TPQ BENEFITS
for all questions, comments (anonymous), standard deviation among team members (a function of team alignment), executive summary charts, and a quadrant chart. (Optional information displayed: executive summary narrative, industry averages, company averages, team leader's answers compared to the team, comparisons of teams handling similar projects, etc.)	meetings (so members can work on process as well as task) is a team intervention if the discussion is carefully facilitated. This may reduce the need for interventions that are perceived as "taking my people away from their jobs."
Results are provided to team members in the form of "spidergrams," which represent clusters of members' responses to each question.	Graphic displays provide an immediate picture of what team members perceive to be happening. These indications of agreement and disagreement among team members have implications for team process effectiveness.
Results from many teams can be combined into a "dashboard" for senior executives to view both processes and productivity.	Team process is likely the leading edge of productivity change within organizations. Senior executives need this information to improve their decision-making and to determine the effects of their policies.

Part IV
Resources

Blanding, Michael, *Cultural Disharmony Undermines Workplace Creativity*, Harvard Business School Working Knowledge Magazine, 09 Dec 2013

Davison, S., C., *Leading and Facilitating International Teams*, Cross Cultural Team Building, Berger, M., McGraw- Hill, 1996

De Mooij, M., *Consumer Behavior and Culture: Consequences for Global Marketing and Advertising*, Sage Publications, Thousand Oaks, CA, 2004

De Mooij, M., *Global Marketing and Advertising: Understanding Cultural Paradoxes (Second Edition)*, Sage Publications, Thousand Oaks, CA, 2005

Distefano, J. J., Maznecski, M. I., *Creating Value with Diverse Team in Global Management*, Organizational Dynamics, Vol. 29, No. 1, pp. 45–63, 2000

Duarte, D. L., and Snyder, N. T., *Mastering Virtual Teams: Strategies, Tools, and Techniques that Succeed*, San Francisco, California, Josey-Bass, 1999

Gannon, M., *Understanding Global Cultures: Metaphorical Journeys Through 28 Nations, Clusters of Nations, and Continents*, Sage Publications, Thousand Oaks, CA, 2004

Granered, E., *Global Call Centers: Achieving Outstanding Customer Service Across Cultures and Time Zones*, Nicholas Brealey International, Boston, MA, 2005

Haywood, M., *Managing Virtual Teams: Practical Techniques for High-technology Project Managers*, San Francisco, California, Boston, MA, Artech House, 1998

Hofstede, G., Hofstede G. J., and Minkov, M., *Culture and Organizations: Software of the Mind (Third Edition)*, McGraw Hill, New York, 2010

Hofstede G. J. and Pederson, P., *Exploring Culture: Stories and Synthetic Cultures*, Intercultural Press, Yarmouth, ME, 2002

Katzenbach. J.R., and Smith, D. K., *The Wisdom of Teams: Creating a High Performance Organization*, HarperBusiness, New York, NY, 2006

Mahal, A., *Facilitator's and Trainer's Toolkit*, Technics Publications, Basking Ridge, NJ, 2014

Parker, G., *Cross Functional Teams: Working with Allies, Enemies, and Other Strangers*, Jossey-Bass, 1992

Rosinski, P., *Coaching Across Cultures: New Tools for Leveraging National, Corporate and Professional Differences*, Nicholas Brearly Publishing, London, 2009

Stahl, Günter K; Maznevski, Martha L; Voigt, Andreas; Jonsen, Karsten, *Unraveling the effects of cultural diversity in teams: A meta-analysis of research on multicultural work groups*, Journal of International Business Studies 41, 690-709 (May 2010) | doi:10.1057/jibs.2009.85

Tough, Allen. T*he Adult's Learning Projects: A fresh approach to theory and practice in adult learning* (Research in education series), Ontario Institute for Studies in Education, 1971

Usczco, G.E., *Tools for Team Excellence: Getting Your Team into High Gear and Keeping it There*, Davis-Black Publishing, Palo Alto, CA, 1996

Bold page numbers indicate definitions